DAVID ADJAYE HOUSES

Dedicated to my mother and father, Cecilia and Afram
my brother, Emmanuel
and Michael Robbins
In memory of Professor Inada, Tokyo

DAVID
ADJAYE
HOUSES

RECYCLING**RECONFIGURING**RE**BUILDING**

Edited by Peter Allison

With 430 illustrations, 162 in colour

 **Thames & Hudson**

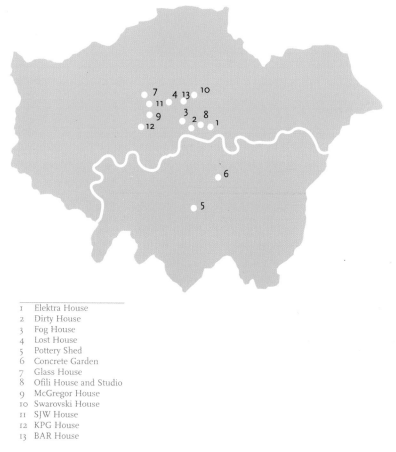

Contents

PORTRAIT OF DAVID ADJAYE BY CHRISTOPH KLAUKE

NEGOTIATING ARCHITECTURE
Stuart Hall

Focusing on the concept of the house and the recycling, or reconfiguring, of interior space, this volume offers a new selection of work from David Adjaye's many-sided, rapidly evolving and strikingly innovative architectural project. 'Project' may be the wrong word, since it suggests linear progression, successive achievement, an evolutionary model. The evidence seems to suggest that not only has Adjaye not acquired some absolute architectural ideal, final identity or signature, but he has also never aimed for such things. Instead, a distinctive practice is everywhere already, unmistakably and insistently present.

One critical element driving Adjaye is his ambition to develop what he calls 'an artist's sensibility' towards the lived-in and built environment. He has been working from the beginning (and is still only 38!) at the frontier between art practice and architecture. Each of his designs represents another sketch, or essay, in this unsettled territory. This has manifestly influenced Adjaye's thinking about how his interior and domestic space is not just about reconceptualizing or designing new kinds of spaces for artists, such as Chris Ofili, Tim Noble and Sue Webster, Jim Casebere and Lorna Simpson, Lubna Chowdhary, Melanie Swarovski and Juergen Teller, to live, work and exhibit in. It has gone one step further in bringing the two languages of art and architecture together through a set of intimate collaborations with artists. Examples are the brilliantly lit chapel and eerie wooden passageway for Ofili's Upper Room, the remodelled red, green and black walls and ceiling of the British pavilion for Ofili's *Paradise Now* at the 2003 Venice Biennale and, most recently, the designs for Faisal Abdu' Allah's *Garden of Eden* at the Chisenhale Gallery.

Paradoxically, the art lies not in some staged aesthetic or the desire to be singularly creative, but in the way each work is rigorously thought through. Emotive architecture, impacting the senses and feelings, it certainly is. First and foremost, however, it is a conceptually driven practice; Adjaye's buildings do not aspire to become artworks. By contrast, they are often halfway to becoming fortified redoubts, scaled-down warehouses, workshops or storage depots. He prefers the metaphor of art to that of architecture, because art, in its contemporary forms, is to him more conceptually rigorous and 'clean'. '[Art] thinks things through more clearly...Architecture takes on too much convention and baggage.' This may be a fond illusion: can anything be less rigorous than the loosely conceptualized conceptualism of so much contemporary art? But, nonetheless, it is an illusion that is working for him.

Eclectic and pluralistic, Adjaye's work draws on diverse influences from architectural practice around the world. His is a hybrid, nomadic, diasporic architecture, shaped and de-centred by a short lifetime of negotiating between different cultures. 'I've had to negotiate culture being a Christian boy in a Muslim country, then an African boy in North London....I was born negotiating.' It is a negotiation informed by an eye that has looked hard and seriously at dwellings, building styles, forms, materials and traditions in North and East Africa, the Middle East and Japan, absorbing and assimilating ideas everywhere without ever falling into a studied vernacular. Currently, the North African elements figure as most influential, defining the repertoire to which Adjaye regularly returns. The recurring corridors in his work – the pathway to Ofili's Upper Room, the Asymmetric Chamber installation for CUBE Gallery, the LxWxH installation on the Rivington Street site of the new inIVA/Autograph arts centre in Shoreditch – remind him of the Moroccan street. Elektra and Dirty houses bring to mind the mud dwelling and the Berber house: thick, dark walls or heavily walled exteriors with eyelets and apertures of brilliant interior light. These are his *Ur*-forms.

Whilst being thoroughly steeped in and at home with modern Western architecture, constantly remaking and tampering with Modernism's essential clean line and white cube, Adjaye has studiously evaded any overarching grand narrative, eschewing the search for that singular mastery of structure and function that characterizes so much of architectural Modernism. Assimilationist and anti-foundational by temper, Adjaye is committed to the more fragmentary character of modern urban life – the fluid, diverse, inclusive, flexible, multi-use, contradictory, transparent – where his houses are most at home. His living spaces, without the imposition of any fixed principles, are thoroughly contemporary – manifestly thought in and for their time and place – whilst avoiding the false trails, the decorative pastiches and the empty quotations of architectural Postmodernism. Adjaye's is a vernacular-inspired modernity.

His forms appear completely in place in the mixed environments of the contemporary city, with its dirt and grime, its secluded enclaves, boarded-up frontages and dangerous corners, its reconditioned warehouses, its parking lots, its cafés, store fronts and showrooms. His buildings fit into this shifting landscape of reconfigured and regenerated urban space without succumbing to it.

They simultaneously belong to and diverge from their context. Bold and seductive by turns, his buildings are like an argument or a proposition that you do not have to like to engage in. Adjaye is an architect of strong, powerful contrasts. His architecture not only lives with but is positively driven by its contradictions: elegance and grime, lightness and grit, weight and weightlessness and, above all, light and dark, glass and chocolate-coloured fudge.

Against the grain of the modern aesthetic, Adjaye has decisively disconnected exterior and interior, flying in the face of the form-and-function orthodoxy. The sealed, sludge-like ramparts and shuttered form of Elektra House [pp 12–25], turned sightlessly and blankly towards the external world and refusing to be penetrated, belie its expansive glass wall, the unexpected apertures and chimney shafts that flood its inside with light. The fortified roughcast exterior and mirrored-glass windows of Dirty House [pp 26–41] are betrayed by the luminous studio spaces and the recessed glass walls of the upper pavilion and the suspended roof, looking across the street to new urban vistas. Nothing in the way these buildings inhabit exterior space prepares us for the reconfigurations of light, textures and spatial relationships that define their interiors.

This flexibility of approach or philosophy is also apparent in the materials used: cheap decking, aluminium panelling, lacquered chipboard, slate, metal and glass sheet, exposed wood and poured concrete. Adjaye wears lightly his technical sophistication; his sketches in space are experimental without being insubstantial or provisional. The 'tech' is low, not high. Its purpose lies not in displaying how his designs work as brilliant technical solutions but in producing a series of effects, at once conceptual and sensuous. An architecture of twists and turns, then, which surprises us, catches our expectations of house and home in an unguarded moment, stages a sort of argument with us about them and takes us somewhere else. Above all, this is a bold, arresting and legible architecture, courageous in its contrasts, in its willingness to live with the contradictions and to make something coherent out of them.

Where does Adjaye's project go next? Normally, this would be a uselessly

Elektra House

project | 1998–2000
total floor area | 110 SQ. M./1184 SQ. FT.
location | WHITECHAPEL, LONDON

STANDING ON A SITE previously occupied by a single-storey workshop [above right], Elektra House still has several references to the earlier building. The height of the front façade is the same as the neighbouring houses but it has the appearance of a single-storey structure, like its predecessor. As in the original building, the house is entered by a side passage and makes extensive use of rooflights. Behind the site is a parking court surrounded by private gardens; looking out from within the house, this is largely hidden by a continuous brick wall.

MODEL, FRONT VIEW

MODEL, BACK VIEW

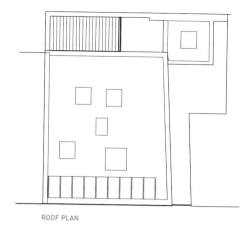

ROOF PLAN

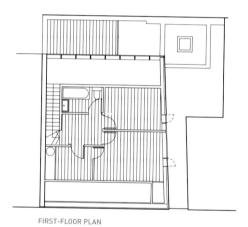

FIRST-FLOOR PLAN

Conceived as a large-scale light box, the building has no conventional windows. From the irregularly shaped entrance passage, an outward-opening door leads into a double-height space, which is flooded with light. The main living area has a lower ceiling and more subdued lighting, but its back wall is gently illuminated by a rooflight above a double-height space [p. 22, right]. After the openness of the ground floor, the first floor is laid out as a series of separate rooms, again lit by rooflights. The only view of the surrounding area is from the top of the staircase, where one can look through the curtain wall that forms the top half of the back façade.

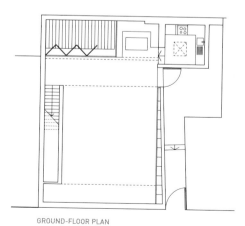

GROUND-FLOOR PLAN

SECTION

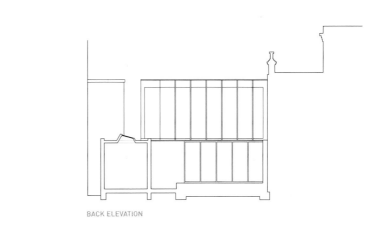

BACK ELEVATION

FRONT ELEVATION

Despite the dark colour of the front and side façades, the physical character of the exterior is light rather than heavy. Most of the construction is hidden from view; on the street façade, the pattern of joints between the panels of resin-faced plywood is the most noticeable detail [overleaf]. Part of the timber frame that supports these panels can be seen on the back façade, standing behind the vertical joints of the curtain wall. At a larger scale, the timber walls and floors are supported by a steel frame whose legs, like a table, stand back from the edges of the site. Towards the street, the unbroken plane of the façade draws attention to that section of the street and the scale of the panels hints at the rhythm of the missing windows [above top].

The clients for Elektra House were two artists, with small children, who wanted to be able to use the living space for the display of art. With its generous width and top-lighting, the space behind the front façade was intended for this purpose [above left]. The possibility of transforming the ground floor into an exhibition space is supported by several details: the concrete floor, a storage wall and the recessed lighting to each side of the boarded ceiling. By comparison, the first floor has a high ceiling, with full-height doors, and there are interesting views of the neighbouring property's side wall [opposite].

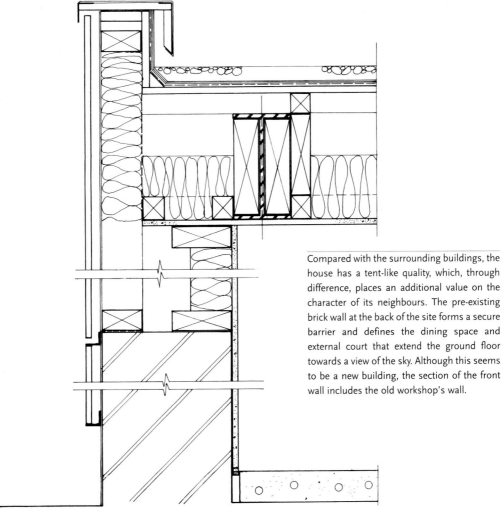

Compared with the surrounding buildings, the house has a tent-like quality, which, through difference, places an additional value on the character of its neighbours. The pre-existing brick wall at the back of the site forms a secure barrier and defines the dining space and external court that extend the ground floor towards a view of the sky. Although this seems to be a new building, the section of the front wall includes the old workshop's wall.

DETAIL OF CONSTRUCTION

Dirty House

project | 2001–02
total floor area | 350 SQ.M./3766 SQ. FT.
location | SHOREDITCH, LONDON

DIRTY HOUSE AND STUDIO occupy the remains of a small factory on a side street in Shoreditch. The majority of openings in the older building have been reused but the balance between solid and void has been altered, in favour of solid, by extending the walls upwards to form a parapet on the top floor.

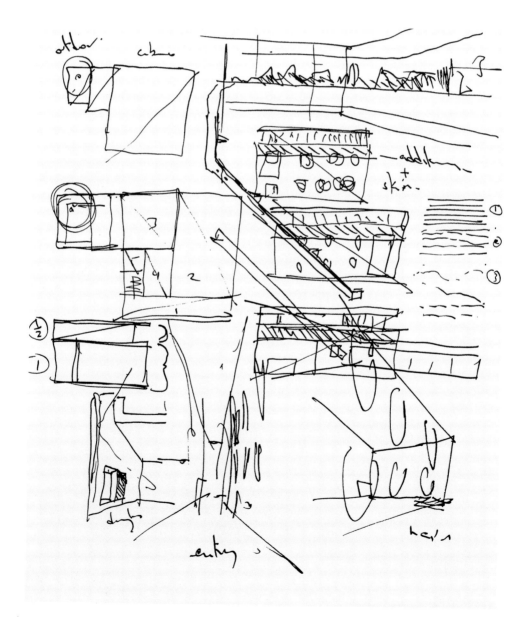

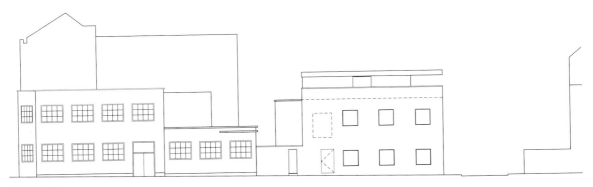

WEST ELEVATION

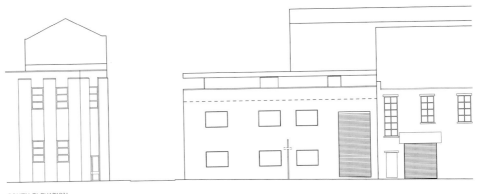

SOUTH ELEVATION

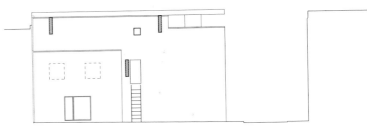

NORTH ELEVATION

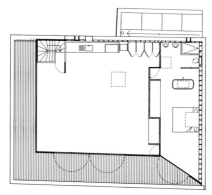

SECOND-FLOOR PLAN

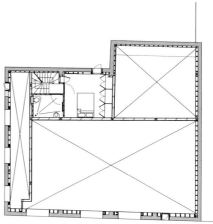

FIRST-FLOOR PLAN

The owners are two artists, Sue Webster and Tim Noble, who needed purpose-designed studio space and a place to live. To avoid any sense of tedium through living and working in the same environment, the two types of accommodation are quite separate and their spatial organization completely different. The studio spaces occupy the volume of the older building in an *en filade* arrangement that is entered through a tall lobby. With tinted reflective glass, the studios are private from the street [p. 33, bottom left]. On the top floor, the living space holds a central position and is surrounded on three sides by a roof terrace and the main bedroom [pp 38–40].

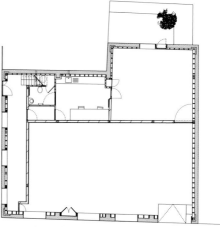

GROUND-FLOOR PLAN

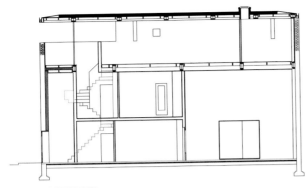

SECTION THROUGH LOBBY

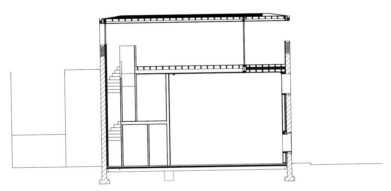

SECTION THROUGH STUDIO 1

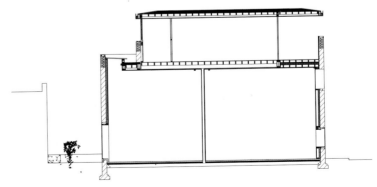

SECTION THROUGH STUDIOS 1 & 2

The interior organization is reflected on the exterior in the contrast between the floating plane of the roof and the solidity of the studio walls. This effect is heightened by the light colour of the roof and by the application of an anti-vandal paint to all external surfaces (except the windows) on the lower floors of the building.

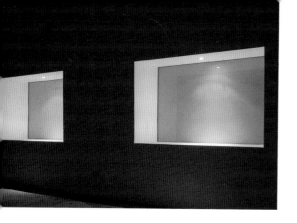

The volume of the main studio is animated by the pattern of sunlight admitted through the windows on the south façade and doorways positioned in diagonally opposite corners [opposite bottom and above left]. With its rooflight, the smaller studio is more vertical in character and is connected to a courtyard at the back of the site [above]. The dividing wall between the studios provides additional stiffness to the floor above.

The horizontal continuity of the residential floor is underlined by the use of external timber decking in all areas. To mitigate against the possibility of splinters, the decking was specially planed for use in the living area and bedroom and white paint was rubbed into the grain of the exposed surface. The same material was also used to clad the inside face of the parapet, whose section incorporates strip lighting that reflects off the floor and onto the underside of the roof.

Located on the inside face of the external walls, the columns of the new steel structure reinforce the existing walls and support the top floor. There is also a new layer of thermal insulation and the resulting increase in wall thickness is visible in the greater depth of the window openings [opposite]. The openness of the living area is complemented by the containment of the main bedroom, although both spaces make use of rooflights to augment the level of natural light in the depth of the section. As the position of the strip lights suggests, the 12mm-wide and 65mm-deep steel mullions distribute the load of the roof to the lower section of the building.

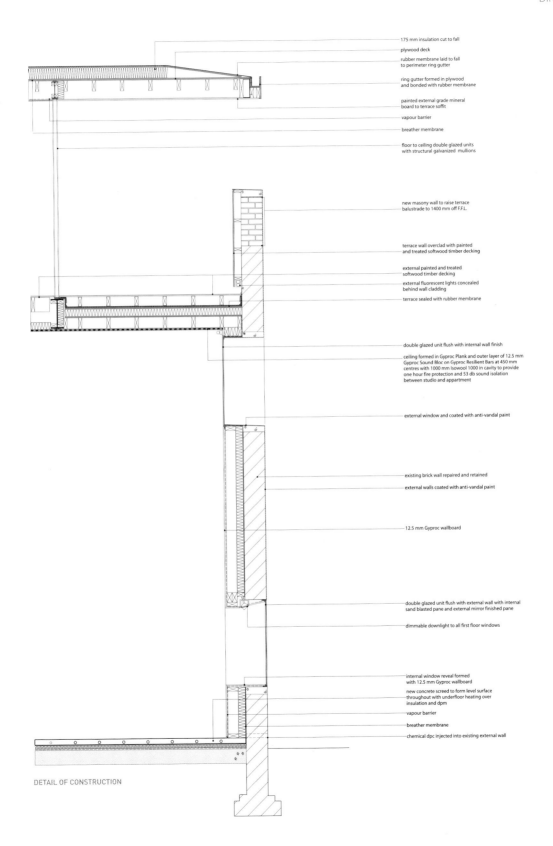

175 mm insulation cut to fall

plywood deck

rubber membrane laid to fall
to perimeter ring gutter

ring gutter formed in plywood
and bonded with rubber membrane

painted external grade mineral
board to terrace soffit

vapour barrier

breather membrane

floor to ceiling double glazed units
with structural galvanized mullions

new masony wall to raise terrace
balustrade to 1400 mm off F.F.L.

terrace wall overclad with painted
and treated softwood timber decking

external painted and treated
softwood timber decking

external fluorescent lights concealed
behind wall cladding

terrace sealed with rubber membrane

double glazed unit flush with internal wall finish

ceiling formed in Gyproc Plank and outer layer of 12.5 mm
Gyproc Sound Bloc on Gyproc Resilient Bars at 450 mm
centres with 1000 mm Isowool 1000 in cavity to provide
one hour fire protection and 53 db sound isolation
between studio and appartment

external window and coated with anti-vandal paint

existing brick wall repaired and retained

external walls coated with anti-vandal paint

12.5 mm Gyproc wallboard

double glazed unit flush with external wall with internal
sand blasted pane and external mirror finished pane

dimmable downlight to all first floor windows

internal window reveal formed
with 12.5 mm Gyproc wallboard

new concrete screed to form level surface
throughout with underfloor heating over
insulation and dpm

vapour barrier

breather membrane

chemical dpc injected into existing external wall

DETAIL OF CONSTRUCTION

Fog House

project | 2002–04
total floor area | 260 SQ. M./2798 SQ. FT.
location | CLERKENWELL, LONDON

WEST ELEVATION

NORTH ELEVATION

A CHAPTER IN Peter Ackroyd's book, *London: The Biography*, is devoted to Clerkenwell, and the Fog House occupies one of the small manufacturing buildings Ackroyd describes as typical of the area. The house is a steel and glass envelope standing inside the shell of the earlier building. Responding to the location, the envelope projects above the shell, offering a view across Clerkenwell's rooftops and towards the parish church, whose churchyard has become a small park.

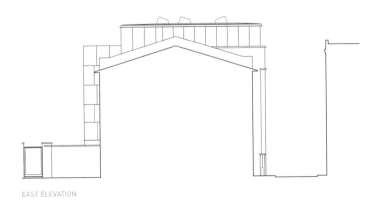

EAST ELEVATION

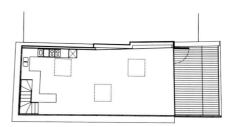

THIRD-FLOOR PLAN

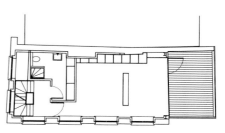

SECOND-FLOOR PLAN

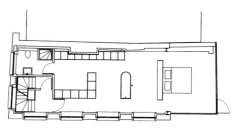

FIRST-FLOOR PLAN

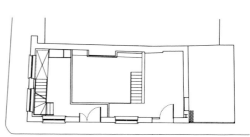

GROUND-FLOOR PLAN

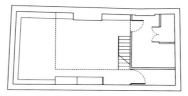

BASEMENT PLAN

The horizontal and vertical projections of the envelope take different forms. Apart from sharing a party wall with the neighbouring property, the living space is a free-standing pavilion with a long side positioned against a brick parapet. Due to a legal difficulty in constructing foundations at the end of the site, the horizontal extension involves a substantial cantilever. In elevation, the sides of the top floor and the horizontal extension are on the same plane. The plans explore the archaeology of the site, masking irregularities in some cases and developing them in others. The latter option is explored in the splayed plan of the top floor.

LONG SECTION

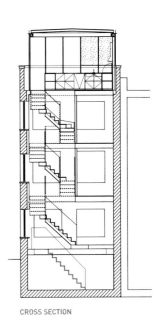

CROSS SECTION

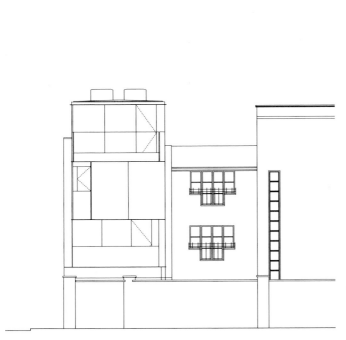

SOUTH ELEVATION

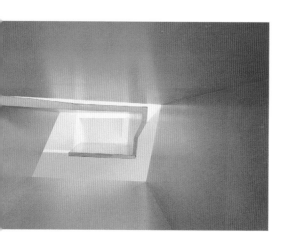

All the windows in the shell have been reglazed with translucent glass so they admit light without giving a view. The intensity of light depends on the distance from the ground and the orientation of the windows; this is especially clear when using the MDF staircase situated on an outside corner, which has windows in two directions. On each of the main floors, the translucent glazing makes a connection between the arrival point and the view towards St James's church, which is framed in a different way on each level [right, pp 53, 55]. The first floor study opens onto a wide terrace [right], forming a loggia overlooking the churchyard.

The outer edge of the horizontal extension is situated directly above the site boundary and Building Regulations require the construction to have a one-hour fire rating. For this reason, a roll-down fire shutter is housed in the bench seat on the upper terrace [p. 55, bottom]. In the event of fire, it would drop into position behind the glazed wall of the bedroom below. The steel and glass side wall of the bedroom is continuous with the pavilion above and the street side of the terrace below.

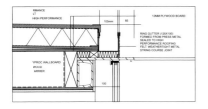

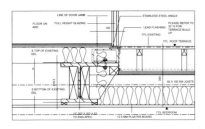

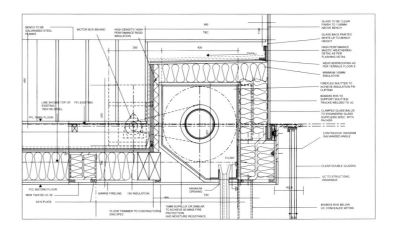

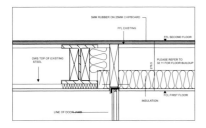

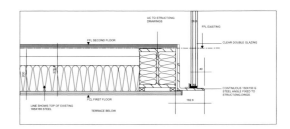

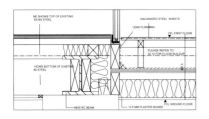

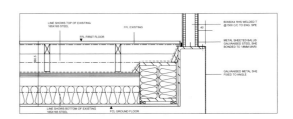

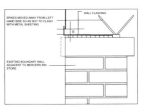

DETAILS OF CONSTRUCTION

A tendency to polarize the edges of each floor is most clear in the main living space, where a panoramic view of the parish church contrasts with a telescopic view of nearby roofs and a gentle splay on the party wall contrasts with the strict linearity of the new wall opposite. The precise colouring of this new wall, and of the space, is dependent on external conditions: in bright weather, it glows with diffused light; at other times, the glass has a darker colour and the internal reflections describe a virtual space that has mysterious depth. The effect of the solid parapet behind this wall is comparable to that of the horizon in a Hiroshi Sugimoto seascape.

Lost House

project | 2002-04
total floor area | 365 SQ. M./3927 SQ. FT.
location | KINGS CROSS, LONDON

THE EAST AND WEST fronts of the Alaska building were at one time connected by a drive-through delivery yard with a solid platform along one edge, against which vehicles parked. For protection from the weather, the parking strip and platform were recessed into the section of the Alaska building above. In Lost House, the parking strip is occupied by two bedrooms [p. 68] and a sunken cinema [p. 66, top], while the platform supports the concrete basin of a lap pool [p. 71, bottom]. The living space occupies the rest of the yard.

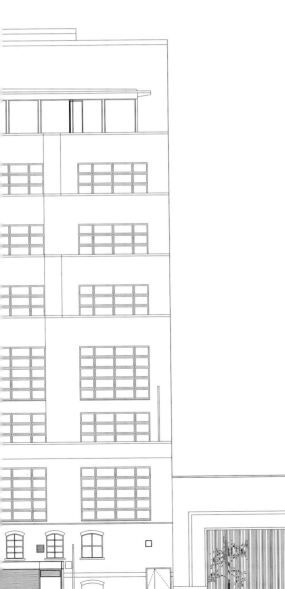

EAST ELEVATION

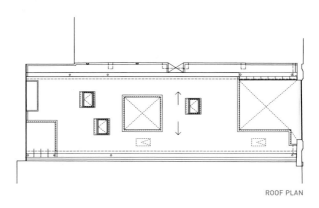

ROOF PLAN

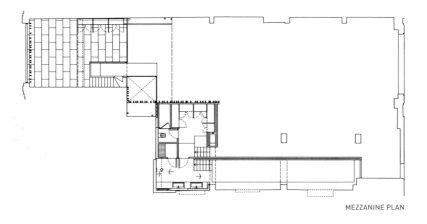

MEZZANINE PLAN

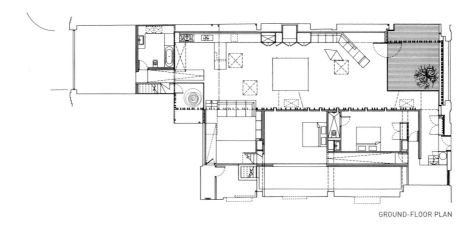

GROUND-FLOOR PLAN

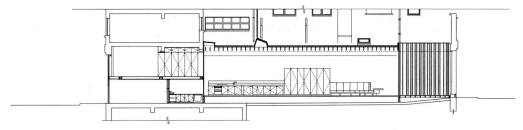

LONG SECTION LOOKING NORTH

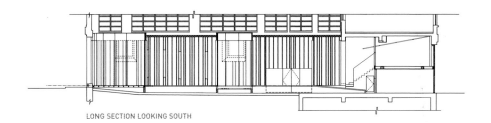

LONG SECTION LOOKING SOUTH

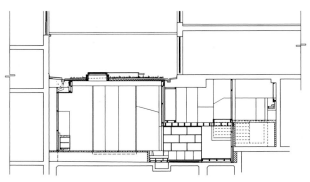

SECTION THROUGH SUNKEN CINEMA

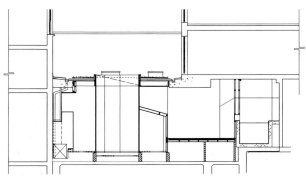

SECTION THROUGH MAIN BEDROOM

Belying its position at the bottom of a light well, Lost House is arranged as an expansive single-storey dwelling with a variety of internal and external views. The positions of the three parallel spaces described by the section of the delivery yard are both reinforced and broken down by the detailed organization of the house; the walls marking the edge of each zone include a range of openings that make a series of transverse connections. To bring light into the deep section, the roof is punctuated by three courtyards and several rooflights, and the wall between the living space and the bedrooms includes a number of slit windows, which filter natural light in one direction and artificial light in the other.

Each of the courtyards has a different size and purpose. The front garden, located immediately behind the rear façade of the Alaska building, will be planted with an olive tree and is large enough to be used for barbecues. The water garden occupies a central position and the surface of the pool will be at the same level as the black resin floor that surrounds it, reflecting light into the interior. Both sides of the living space can be used for circulation: to the south, the route connects the entrance area, continuing under two light scoops, with the steps into the sunken cinema; to the north, the route is defined by a continuous element that has the kitchen at one end, storage in the middle and seating at the other end [pages 64, 65]. As the clients work in the fashion industry, the south side can also be used as a catwalk.

The spatial layering of the plan is reinforced by the use of colour. In the living space, the bedroom wall and the ceiling are stained black to match the floor, while the kitchen, storage and seating areas are in a range of earthy colours [below left]. Behind the bedroom wall, each volume is a different colour with matching carpet [opposite]. For acoustic reasons, the floor and screen wall in the sunken cinema are lined with carpet. The back garden [below] will be landscaped with a small mound of black gravel and planted with herbs.

In contrast to the exposed construction in the living area, the walls of the bedrooms are only broken by doorways, windows and light scoops that admit light from the nearest court. Occupying a central position, the main bedroom enjoys long views in each direction and has a horizontal window at the level of the water in the lap pool [p. 71].

Due to their location, the ceilings of the bedrooms, bathing and changing areas incorporate concrete brackets and beams to support the building above. The colour scheme and the geometry and detailing of the storage areas unite the volumes with the larger structure that contains them. The lap pool is different from other examples in the history of Modernism: the space is painted mat black and the only natural light is borrowed from the entrance lobby and the bedrooms.

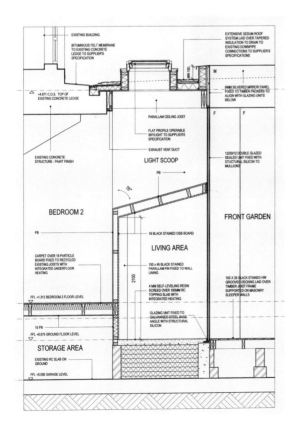

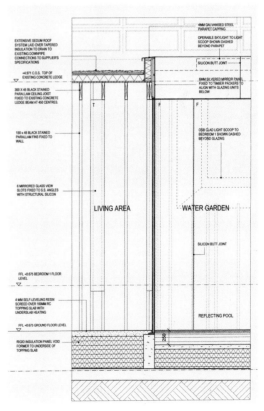

In the living space, as a result of the combination of exposed construction, glazed walls and reflective surfaces, there is a continuous interplay between the solidity of materials and the ephemeral effects of light coming from a variety of sources. In the longer views, it is often difficult to see where the space actually ends, as its considerable length is extended by reflection. Looking into the courtyards, the glass walls and mirrored panels reflect the surrounding buildings, introducing a spatial dimension that is significantly larger than the physical dimensions of the internal space. On many occasions, there is a four-way interaction between Lost House, its reflection, the surrounding buildings and their reflections. The neighbours now look out onto a moss roof and not the old delivery yard.

DETAILS OF CONSTRUCTION

Light and Colour

There is an interesting parallel between Adjaye's approach to colour and the 'blue-bulb theory' of Walter Murch, editor of films by Francis Ford Coppola among others.[1] According to Murch, the last thing a film-maker should include in a scene that requires blue lighting is a blue light, as it would focus attention on the light itself, causing the eye to tense up and not take in the full picture. Instead, the blue light should be positioned out of camera so that the eye is more relaxed and able to appreciate the authentically blue things. All of Adjaye's houses include arrangements that are intended to provide even, glare-free lighting: areas of translucent glazing, multiple rooflights, rooflights above slots of space that reflect light into the area below. Sources of both natural and artificial light are positioned to wash a surface with light and to illuminate the larger space of which they are part. The texture and colour of the surface interact and produce a hybrid plane that is neither material nor light, but a combination of both. Adjaye's understanding of the relationship between light materials and colour has been strongly influenced by the eight months he spent in Japan as a student: 'For me, darkness is a kind of physicality and a colour, and Japan was the first place where I encountered that directly. There is a famous book, *In Praise of Shadows*, and, when you hang out in Gion in the evenings, you realize this idea of darkness. So, there is the perception of materials in daylight and the perception of materials at dusk when they take on a more profound meaning because they are not so naked. They start to play a more spatial role, a sort of theatrical framing. That was very special for me, the idea of light and the way light appears. Light is no longer a bulb but becomes another plane, literally a physical plane.'[2] Apart from his appreciation of the inspirational qualities of timber toilets in the temples of Nara and Kyoto, the author of *In Praise of Shadows*, Jun'ichiro Tanizaki, investigates the significance of shadow and darkness in relation to several aspects of traditional culture: the domestic interior, food, theatre, dress and the Japanese complexion.[3] In his architecture, Adjaye has explored the implications of black as a primary reference in the black exteriors of Elektra, Dirty and Fog houses, in the black exteriors and interiors of BAR and Lost houses and in avoiding the use of white in the non-black projects.

1   Michael Ondaatje, *The Conversations: Walter Murch and the Art of Editing Film* (London: Bloomsbury, 2002): 140–41.
2   David Adjaye, interview with the author, 24 April 2002.
3   Jun'ichiro Tanizaki, *In Praise of Shadows* (English translation, New Haven, CT: Leete's Island Books, 1977). First published in Japanese in 1933.

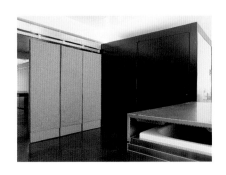

LUNCH @ EXMOUTH MARKET, 1995

LIVING IN RUINS
Peter Allison

In Adjaye's sketches of his houses, one of the elements that appears most often is a solid rectangular tube capable of right-angled turns. As drawn, the tubes' function and scale are ambiguous, but, in reality, they are as long as possible within the space they occupy: the edge of the raised courtyard and seating in Elektra House, the kitchen in Fog House [p. 55, top left] and the external seating and planter in BAR House [p. 231]. With oblique angles, similar drawings could account for the worktop and seating units in BAR and Lost houses [p. 229 and p. 65, bottom]. In each case, the tubular section has a functional justification, the edge conditions change continuously along its length and it can be used at any point, providing a scale of differentiated experiences in the space it occupies. The studies of these barlike elements and their realization demonstrate Adjaye's ability to mask, or edit, distracting detail by including it within a form that is distinguished by its continuity.

A similar principle characterizes the main circulation route in most of the houses. A common goal in domestic architecture is to reduce the amount of space used for circulation to a minimum in order for other areas to be as large as possible. In most of Adjaye's designs, the space available has strict limits due to existing walls, but, nevertheless, it is normal for his circulation to be as long as reasonably possible. With sharp changes of direction, it traverses the dimensions of the available volume, providing a powerful sequence of views in the process; arranged as a loose spiral, the circulation route in Elektra House provides an early example [pp 12–25]. The most elongated route to date is in Lost House [pp 56–73]: taking the swimming pool into account, it is necessary to traverse the length of this single-storey house four complete times to visit all areas.[1] The extended *promenade architecturale* is a feature of Luigi Snozzi's classic houses, which often occupy impressive sites in the Swiss Ticino. Instead of capturing the relationship between the house and the landscape, as in the case of Snozzi, Adjaye's routes explore the volumes of former buildings and their relationship to the city. This is especially true of the multiple views, direct and reflected, along the route of Lost House.

Despite physical incompleteness, ruins have a powerful presence. Empty doors and unglazed windows have the effect of an over-scaled mask, suggesting patterns of occupation without being specific. Over time, the finishes on interior surfaces are often lost, revealing that the basic construction of floors, walls and ceilings had been carried out in the same material. Without finishes and furniture, the proportions of spaces and their connection to one another are surprisingly clear. Often floors have fallen in leaving half-complete interiors reached by low flights of stairs; their handrails have long since disappeared and there is an element of risk in using them. The stages of decay in different locations provide a demonstration, in reverse, of how such buildings were constructed and, lacking the details carried out in less resilient materials, the essential characteristics of their organization are more legible than they would have been in their prime.

Inhabiting the footprint, if not the actual shell, of older buildings, Adjaye's houses rub shoulders with the phenomenon of ruins from their inception. With the intention of continuing where time left off, Adjaye takes advantage of modern technology to continue the process that history set in motion. Windows do not have frames, being detailed as lengths of transparent wall; doors open to the underside of roofs; half-levels and parapets suggest the possibility of a further view; solid ventilation panels look like replacements for conventional windows that were broken at some time in the past. Internally, the same material is used to finish most, if not all, of the surfaces in a single space, and the legibility of each volume is maintained by the provision of storage walls for the belongings of the current occupants. In this way, there is a high degree of continuity between old and new work, without any confusion about which is which. The remains of the old work are the subject of restoration and their own special finishes, such as black paint, while the new work makes full use of contemporary materials. The sense of two partial buildings, old and new, working together is particularly clear when looking at the back façade of Swarovski House [p. 177].

During his time in Japan, Adjaye spent two months sweeping and measuring a teahouse whose materials consisted of a shaved birch branch, paper, render and tatami mats. Despite their poor quality, they were capable of controlling space in a precise way and, as an ensemble, had considerable presence. He was also attending lectures on Buddhist philosophy and made a connection between the type of emancipation that comes from standing back from the concerns of every-day life and the architecture of the teahouse. He 'experienced a sense of release from the expectations linked with a conventional understanding of materiality and realized that it was possible to have a more willed position that is not to do with materials but with the ability to bring certain conditions together to make spatial ideas, form ideas'.[2] Looking at some of Adjaye's more luxurious houses, with

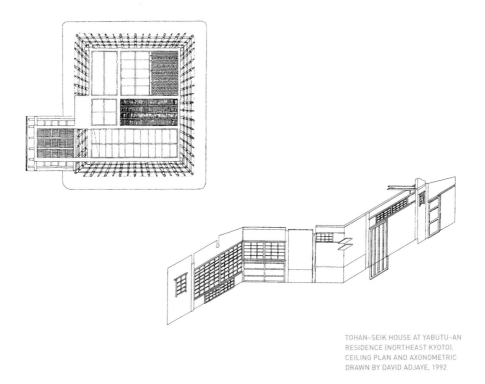

expanses of stone and expensive joinery, one might be excused for thinking that they demonstrate a conventional understanding of materiality. So where are the spatial ideas to which he alludes?

The basic module of space in Adjaye's houses has something in common with a two-person tent: from the outside, it only seems big enough for one whilst, inside, it looks as if it could almost take three. As inside a tent, the floor may be a different material but the remaining surfaces have the same finish and an identical colour, and it is not clear how they are held in position. These principles apply in Adjaye's work regardless of the simplicity or complexity of the volume in question and the experience of enlargement is effective at all scales. In Elektra House we experience a sense of release in the top-lit bedrooms; the basement living space is larger than anything one might expect from looking at the front of Swarovski House; and the floating interiors of Dirty House contradict the external façades in both volume and complexity. In each case, the surface qualities of the

HARBOUR AND ROOM, 1932–36, PAUL NASH, © TATE, LONDON 2005

materials provide an experience that is directly related to the use of the space; they do not celebrate the character of the materials for their own sake. Luxury may be a possibility for wealthy clients, but Adjaye's approach does not depend on it, as shown in Pottery Shed [pp 90–99].

The small interior giving an experience of a larger space could, of course, be a teahouse, and an extension of this strategy in Adjaye's work concerns the interior that could be an exterior. The ground floor of Elektra House is entirely open between the front and back walls of the site, both of which are painted white and lit from above. As the conditioning of the internal and external walls is identical, it is unclear whether the single space, in which the walls have equivalent roles, should be considered an interior or an exterior. A similar ambiguity occurs in Swarovski House where, apart from its size, the basement living space is lined with a material that is more readily associated with cladding the outside of a house. The type of lighting produced by rooflights is reminiscent of the light in external spaces and this is particularly true when several rooflights are used together, as in the living spaces of Dirty and Fog houses. In both cases, the techniques used effectively create no difference between the appearance of the inside and the outside: in Dirty House, the same flooring is used for the terrace and the living space; in Fog House, the reflection of the living space in the external wall is comparable to the experience of reflections on the outside of glass buildings. The result of this type of spatial manipulation is to extend the limits of perception beyond the physical constraints of the site, an achievement that is as enriching as it is surprising.

Adjaye studied advanced-level chemistry at school and it is tempting to suggest that, since that time, he has maintained an interest in controlled explosions. This aspect of his architecture also reverses Le Corbusier's famous definition of architecture as 'the masterly, correct and magnificent play of masses brought together in light' – a significant part of Adjaye's programme involves the dematerialization of form by light. In this connection, the positioning of strip lights in the angles of spaces between walls and ceilings, for instance, is most revealing. When they are lit, the junction between adjacent planes, normally the most rigid part of any structure, dissolves in light.

A persistent tendency in Adjaye's projects is the deliberate polarization of conditions at all scales: outside-inside, public-private, open-closed, transparent-solid. This is combined with practical arrangements that consistently promote the possibility of being drawn into a partial reading of the interaction between such polarities. A physical journey from one extreme to the other is described by the main circulation route, vertically in Swarovski House and horizontally in KPG House [pp 204–21]. There is a visual confrontation between old and new in Swarovski House and between solid and translucent in Fog House. The perception of polar opposites occurs in the reversible relationship between inside and outside in SJW House [pp 192–203] and Pottery Shed. This does not depend on moving from inside to outside, or vice versa, but can be understood equally well from either position. Despite an underlying stability in its geometrical organization, Adjaye's architecture is sprinkled with suggestions of movement: the directional design of handrails, rooflights facing in different directions to distinguish the light falling into the same space, non-regular placement of fins and mullions.[3] With motion of the body, eye or mind, the balance between light and shade, definite and indefinite, reality and illusion, becomes unstable.[4] On this basis, the interior and its relationship to the outside world is capable of various forms of metamorphosis.

During the day, the visual orientation of KPG House is horizontal, towards the external views; at night, as the artificial light in the ceiling and rooflights take over, the spaces are more inward looking and vertical in character. The real view of the Clerkenwell rooftops on the top floor of Fog House is overlaid with a virtual, but no less convincing, view of the interior of the house itself. When Lost House is primarily an interior with a very small exterior, the experience of being inside is conditioned by a multiplicity of periscope-like details of the surrounding buildings. There is a depiction of this type of experience in a painting by Paul Nash (1889–1946), *Harbour and Room* (1932–36, p. 86), which shows the interpenetration of a hotel room and a seascape. As Roland Penrose wrote of Nash's work, 'one reality leads into another with the assurance that both exist simultaneously and in the same place'.[5]

The Poetics of Space by Gaston Bachelard still contains the most comprehensive collection of poetic images from literature relating to the house and the experience of inhabitation, along with extensive analysis. According to Bachelard, the chief benefit of the house is that it 'shelters daydreaming', and the aim of his book is to 'show that the house is one of the greatest powers of integration for the thoughts, memories and dreams of mankind'.[6] From the experience of the light by a certain window, to the house as a refuge from the storms of life, the only limitation of

Bachelard's images is that they refer to traditional houses. Through a combination of strategies, Adjaye's houses support the daydreaming that Bachelard recommends whilst remaining firmly in the present.

1   This arrangement can be seen in non-domestic areas, for instance, shopping malls and the Disney environments.
2   David Adjaye, interview with the author, 24 April 2002.
3   The stability provides a platform for the multiple readings described; without it, there would be nothing but kaleidoscopic effects.
4   Walter Murch describes how the editor of a film should know where the audience's eye will be before and after each cut (Michael Ondaatje, *The Conversations: Walter Murch and the Art of Editing Film*, London: Bloomsbury, 2002, p. 41). There is a similar sense of the eye being guided through Adjaye's houses.
5   Roland Penrose, 'The Transparent Mirror' (*The London Bulletin*, no. 2, May 1938), quoted in Roger Cardinal, *The Landscape Vision of Paul Nash* (London: Reaktion, 1989, p. 90), where *Harbour and Room* is discussed in more detail.
6   Gaston Bachelard, *The Poetics of Space* (New York, NY: Orion Press, 1964): 6. Translated from *La Poétique de l'Espace*, 1958.

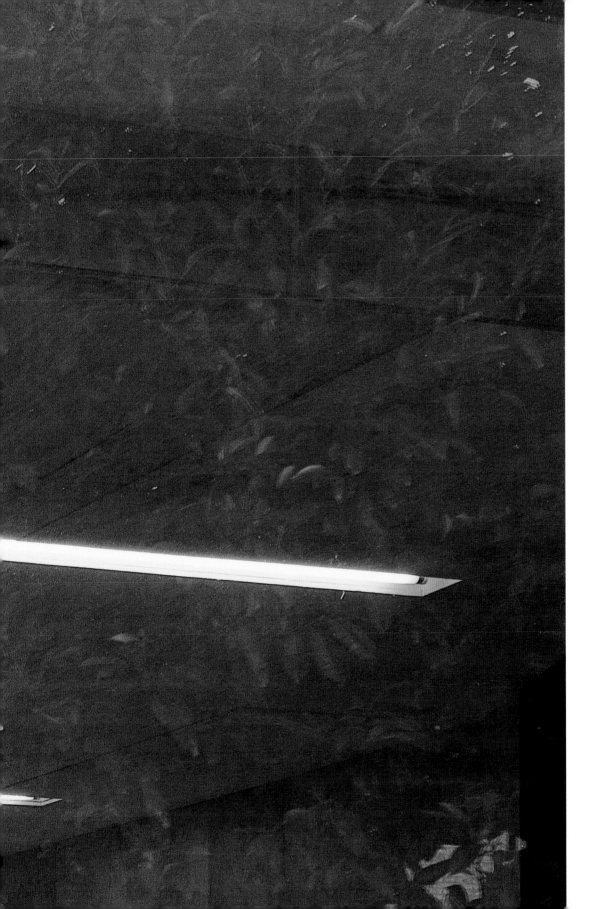

Pottery Shed

project | 2003
total floor area | 26.7 SQ. M./287 SQ. FT.
location | STREATHAM, LONDON

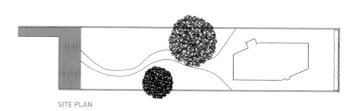

SITE PLAN

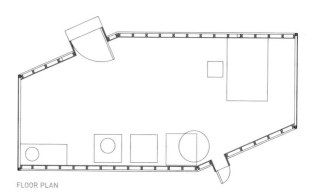

FLOOR PLAN

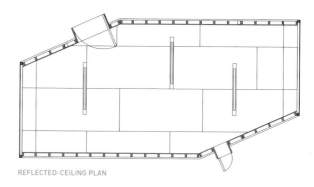

REFLECTED-CEILING PLAN

THIS IS A SHED in spirit only. Like a shed, it is clear what it is, where it stands and from what it is made. Unlike a shed, it has a flat roof, chamfered corners, very large windows and one can see straight through it. Surrounded by fences, shrubs and trees, its nearest neighbour is another shed; in this setting, the special attributes of Pottery Shed are unlikely to pass without notice.

The existing garden path is made from irregular paving slabs, loosely slotted together, and its route makes a series of angled adjustments from one side of the garden to the other. The chamfered corners of the new shed continue this pattern and support the design in other ways. By diminishing the section towards the view, they increase the sense of separation between outside and inside; their displacement on opposite walls helps to define the two areas for practical work and study required by the client and they counteract the lack of cross-sectional stiffness that can be a weakness in tube structures.

The construction of Pottery Shed follows a familiar pattern. There is a strong contrast between the colour and materiality of exterior and interior and an equivalent level of concern for the continuity of surface in each case. Internally, the same plywood is used for the floor, walls and ceiling, with no distracting cover strips at the junctions between planes. There are separate ventilation panels so the windows do not need to open and, as a result, the fixing of the glazing can be included in the detailing of the cladding and lining. Lacking a conventional frame, the view in and the view out have equal significance, which means that they are completely reversible.

38mm Ariel Coroline profiled board black
Tyvek breather membrane
100mm mineral wool
18mm plywood

Metal angle to keep Tyvek
sheeting in place

Timber packer painted black

Black powder coated steel angle
75 x 75 x 6mm

Black Enamelled paint to back of glass

DETAIL OF CONSTRUCTION

12mm single glazed unit tbs by
glass contractor
bonded onto steel angle with
structural tape

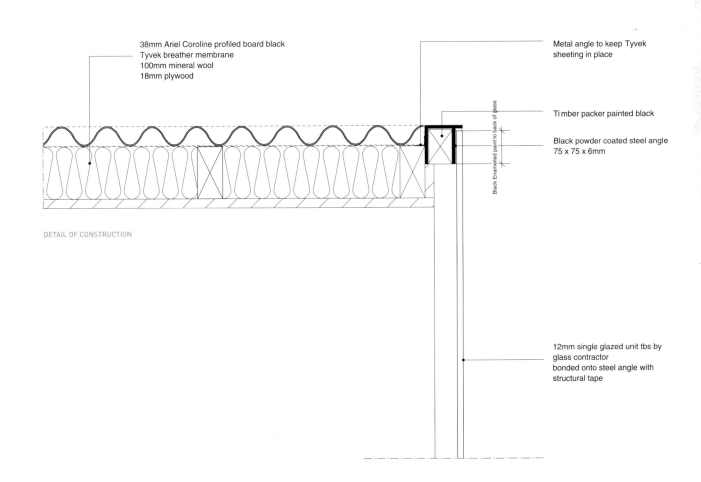

Concrete Garden

project | 2001
total floor area | 48 SQ. M./516 SQ. FT.
location | DULWICH, LONDON

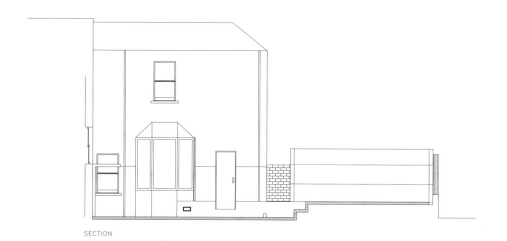

SECTION

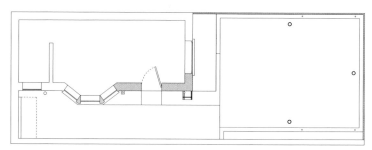

PLAN

THIS PROJECT INVERTS the normal concept of a garden as an area of planting, where the edge condition is of little importance, by constructing an empty space enclosed by a continuous concrete wall, 2.2m high. Spaces that can be seen but not necessarily entered can be found in traditional and contemporary architecture in Japan. They provide occasions when normal perceptions of scale and convention are suspended and the emptiness itself draws attention to the scale and materiality of the enclosure and to the subtle changes of atmosphere depending on the season, the weather or the time of day.

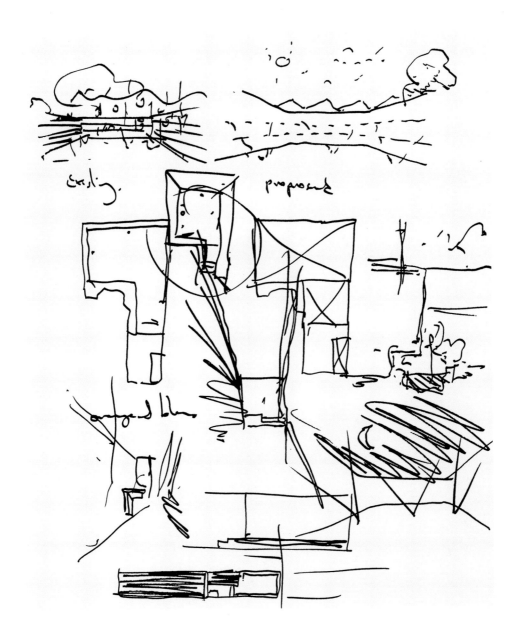

The colour of the walls is the result of adding rust to the concrete before it was placed in position. In sunlight, it is a bright reddish brown [opposite]; in subdued light, it is a more recessive shade [p. 105]. Apart from the walls' ability to focus transient effects, they frame a view of the sky in which details from the surrounding environment are displayed in relative isolation along their bottom edge: chimneys in various states of repair, the tops of trees, areas of brickwork. Removed from their normal context, these details have a clarity of form and structure that might otherwise go unnoticed. The height of the walls is the maximum allowed without obtaining planning permission.

Glass House

project | 2001–02
total floor area | 221 SQ. M./2379 SQ. FT.
location | HAMPSTEAD, LONDON

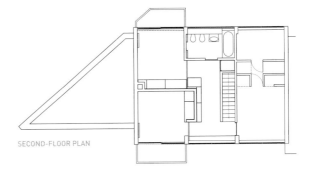

SECOND-FLOOR PLAN

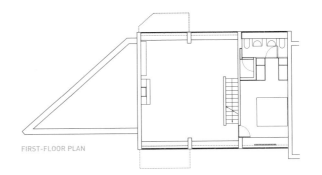

FIRST-FLOOR PLAN

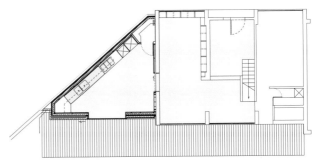

GROUND-FLOOR PLAN

ORIGINALLY DESIGNED BY John Winter and completed in 1970, this house is a fine example of an architecture based on a rational approach to structure and construction. The organization of the interior develops from the geometry of the three structural bays, shown by the divisions between the windows on the main façades, and the main living space is on the first floor. Adjaye/Associates was approached to update the fabric of the original house and to construct a kitchen extension that would enlarge the dining area.

The external walls of the 1970 house were constructed from concrete blocks and clad in ceramic tiles. To improve their thermal performance in 2002, the tiles were removed, a layer of insulation added to the blockwork and the façades reclad using a similar tile to the original. The windows were also replaced on a similar basis. Aside from new front and garage doors, the only change to the main façades is the increased depth of each opening due to the thickness of the new insulation.

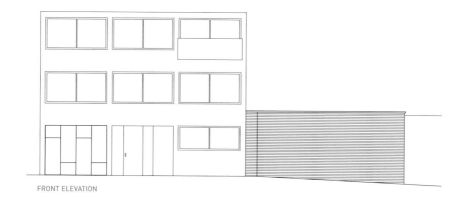

FRONT ELEVATION

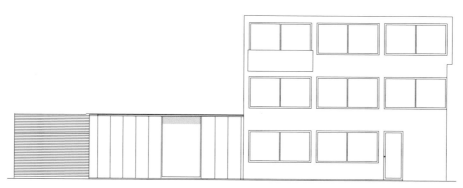

BACK ELEVATION

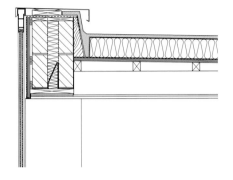

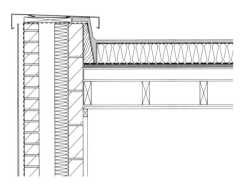

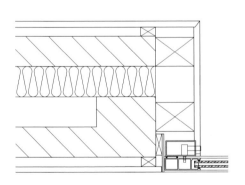

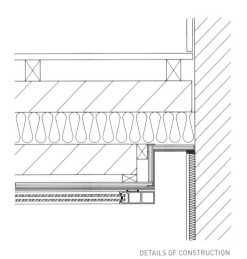

DETAILS OF CONSTRUCTION

The kitchen extension occupies a blind corner next to the main house. The single-storey façade stands slightly back from, but continues the line of, the three-storey façade and both are linked to the garden by a raised boardwalk. Whether open or closed, the new external door strengthens the relationship between the house and garden.

Following John Winter's example, the kitchen extension is a demonstration of a contemporary language of construction. The new façade is built from two types of vertical panels instead of the horizontal perforations of the main house. The interaction between glass as a transparent material and glass as a reflective surface is continued by the sliding door and the three glass panels next to the house. The inner face of these panels has a sprayed enamel finish, while the other panels are made from Eternit board and do not have a reflective surface. When the door is closed, half the façade is reflective; when it is open, this is reduced to a quarter. The panels are the same height as the garden wall that forms the back wall to the kitchen.

Furniture

In the production of a feature-length film, it is normal practice to shoot more scenes than appear in the version that goes on general release. The combination of imagery and sound results in a level of redundant information that makes it possible to complete the story without showing every incident. The implications of the remaining action allow the audience to complete the story for themselves.[1] There is a similar level of redundancy in most houses: a kitchen, for instance, is likely to include a sink, an oven, a hob, a refrigerator and a worktop, all of which reinforce the identity of the space known as 'the kitchen'. In Adjaye's houses, there is a process of editing, analogous to that in film-making, which aims to refresh the plot of residential architecture whilst reducing the information overload that is a normal part of the domestic environment. The staircases in terraced houses are reconfigured to enrich the experience of moving from one floor to another; spaces that might previously have been treated in a similar manner are polarized in their scale and materiality; rooms with views become rooms with light but no view. Instead of the identity of a space being based on the combined effect of its contents, it is primarily determined on the basis of its position within a larger spatial sequence. A sleeping space is defined by its position at the top of a house, in the roof, or by the quality of light coming from above. In this approach, it is helpful if items of furniture are not overburdened with information concerning their location and use. Adjaye's furniture, at all scales, fulfils this requirement by continuing the part-scenographic, part-abstract character of his architecture. A kitchen becomes a concrete beam whose cantilever forms a breakfast bar; a table repeats the structural form of the space it stands in; a stool frames a view, like a doorway. It is not Adjaye's intention, however, that each of his houses should be a *gesamtkunstwerk*. His normal strategy is to design key items of furniture to provide a link between the scale of the architecture and the process of inhabitation. This is a supportive move; beyond this point, the occupants are expected to do exactly as they wish.

---

1   Michael Ondaatje, *The Conversations: Walter Murch and the Art of Editing Film* (London: Bloomsbury, 2002): 46. In a continuation of this discussion, Ondaatje refers to an intriguing quotation from Miles Davis: 'I listen to what I can leave out'.

P. *119:* side table, 1999
Clockwise, from top:
table/chair/storage/stool, 1995
lightback chair, 1994
side chairs, 1993

Clockwise, from top:
stool, 1997
high stool, 1998
bench/magazine rack, 1999

Clockwise, from top left:
bench, 1995
steps, 1999
side table, 1998
trolley, 1999

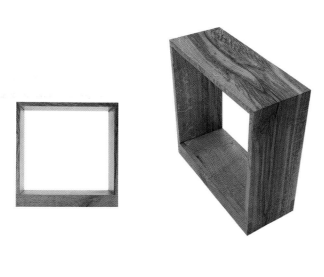

Opposite: sauna chair, 2000
Below: bed, 1995

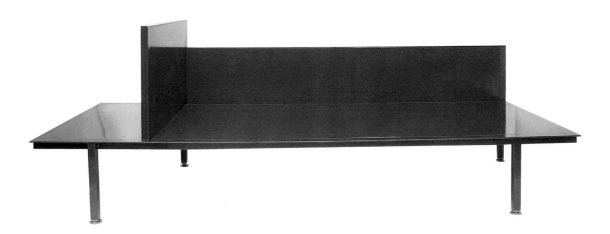

Clockwise, from top left:
bench, 1998
worktable, 1997
daybed, 1996
table, 1998

Worktable, 1999

THE TALE OF A HOUSE
Caroline Roux

This is a story that begins in London's East End and finishes at Tate Modern, locations not so very far apart in miles, but a long way in terms of ambition. It starts in Brick Lane – where shop windows are heaped with garish Asian sweets and curry-house signs flicker – in the summer of 1997 with the artist Chris Ofili.

Though only a few years out of college, Ofili is a rising star in need of a home. He has bought a building – a delightful but dilapidated Huguenot silk-weaver's house on the joyously named Fashion Street, off Brick Lane – but nightly visits reveal it not to be a home at all but a mess. Behind its pretty brick façade is an unusable burden and, while the house crumbles, Ofili is still making the daily commute from a flat in Balham, south London, to a studio overlooking a hookers' playground in Kings Cross.

Ofili cruises past curry places, *corta* tunic shops and beigel bakeries in his lime green Capri. The location, on the fault line between the goldmine of the City and the chaos of inner city, is perfect. He desires to live and work in one space in an active place, and there is plenty going on in this part of town in the late 1990s; it is the eye of London's cultural storm. All the artists are here, their studios scattered among the Bangladeshi cafés, the mosques and the synagogues. He has Jake Chapman on one side and Dinos Chapman on the other. It is good to know your neighbours. They have even been in the same show: Charles Saatchi's 'Sensation' at the Royal Academy. Yet Ofili is uneasy.

You might think that chance encounters are the stuff of fiction, the *fait glissade* of the surrealist novel, the driving narrative force of the Hollywood romance. But, Ofili's sighting of David Adjaye, the young Ghanaian architect who had also been at the Royal College of Art and had set up an office close to Brick Lane with William Russell in 1994, on a summer evening could hardly have been more real, timely or right. Ofili takes Adjaye to see the house and a unique relationship begins.

David Adjaye was no newcomer to recycling old buildings. For a noodle bar, Soba, he had taken a deep space with the possibility of a rooflight, but transformed it with back-lit walls instead. At Lunch, a deli-style café, he adapted a regular narrow shop unit by dropping the floor into the basement, completing the transformation with a large window onto the yard behind. Early domestic work included an apartment with a luminous resin floor but now there were other possibilities in sight, including Elektra House in Whitechapel. This modest house for a family was finally completed in 2000 and stands – alongside Ofili's house – as one of Adjaye's most restrained yet resonant pieces of small-scale architecture.

Ofili's house is, however, an entirely different proposition: a project with no clear architectural game plan, no economic forecasting attached. It is to be driven only by the needs and desires of the owner. The last thing Ofili wants is a show house. He had not even considered getting the help of an architect until the chance encounter with Adjaye, and it is perhaps more appropriate to describe the working relationship between the two as an endless dialogue of increasing revelation, rather than anything resembling a more strategic and formal client-based relationship. What Ofili requires practically is a fully functioning studio and emotionally a refuge. The first flushes of fame are starting to compromise his privacy and he senses that his freedom is slipping away.

'This is a house for someone with a twenty-four-hour obsession and a need for peace. That's the diagram of the house,' says Adjaye now. 'It can be read in many ways, one is as a series of extrusions sitting on top of one another. But really it's a journey from rest to work and back again. It is about lodging the studio – not just physically but in relation to a life. The studio had to be at the back of the house so we could dig down to create a double-height space. But, more importantly, it had to be as diametrically far apart from the sleeping space as the plan would allow.'

This is a house [pp 138–53] for someone who might stay inside it for a month at a time, compelled to paint, needing to eat and sleep, and the plan reflects that. Ofili wanted distinct rooms, spaces that while seamlessly connected clearly express their purpose; a jigsaw of changing mood and pace. 'I work in big open spaces and I need to have intimacy elsewhere.'

Despite its height, the painting studio is almost invisible. Austere and unadorned, like a cross between a Lutheran chapel and an operating theatre with its bare walls and concrete floor, it is a place of dissection and creation. The drawing studio hunkers beneath the pavement lights in the building's front basement. Back then, it felt to Adjaye that Ofili wanted to hide beneath the crowd there, like a child creating a parallel universe beneath the dining table.

In contrast, the first-floor living space with its wooden floor and unpainted plaster is warm and gentle. The slender kitchen flows into an extended terrace. If the studio is all enclosure, the living space is open to the world, inviting the outside in. Up another flight of stairs is a spare room and bathroom, and up once more you reach the quiet luxury of a large room – a lung – lined with wardrobes and with a sleeping platform above. In a space just big enough for a big bed, Adjaye places Ofili as far from the street and as near to the stars as the building will allow. The window, carved out of the touchable roof, tracks the sun and the rising moon, connecting the city dweller to the wider world, where natural rhythms prevail.

At street level, the old shop front has been replaced by a set of milky white glass doors, which can fold away to allow the delivery of big canvasses (Ofili's paintings are often 8 feet tall). The big studio is roofed with glass bricks, filling it with daylight that is never dramatic and always diffused, a soft light in a sharp space. Ofili can start work at six in the evening if he wishes and continue until 3am, whilst keeping a consistency of light with the natural, tungsten and white light on offer. There is a diagonal sight line slicing through the building from the bedroom at the very top down to the bottom corner of the studio. Thus ,within its historic shell, the house is peculiarly porous, uniquely sensitive to Ofili's needs.

To look at other houses Adjaye has made brings the particularity of the house in Fashion Street into focus. Many can be seen as glorious stage sets that address the public and private sides of their clients: artists Tim Noble and Sue Webster's alluring Dirty House [pp 26–41], for example, with its night-time crown of come-hither light and its wide-open white interior; or the twenty-first-century apartment/palace in Kensington Palace Gardens [pp 204–21], for a man of considerable means, with its magnificent stone-lined receiving rooms and its warren of private quarters panelled in exotic veneers. Ofili's house, by contrast, with its raw plaster walls, is quiet, unassuming and almost machine-like in its specificity of arrangement. Only Elektra House [pp 12–25], containing family life behind its perversely blank exterior wall, offers a similar expression of contented privacy and function.

Adjaye has always hankered after the artist's sensibility. It is, he says, why he continued his studies at the Royal College of Art rather than choosing an architectural school. He has collaborated in the past with the artist Henna Nadeem on a public playground for children and with sculptor Mary Evans on a three-dimensional installation. He explains 'You sort of live through them – it's a way of getting the freedom that I ultimately want. When I work with an artist I get close to that freedom, though it's not real. I know that. But it's something I like as a fiction.'

Through Ofili, Adjaye makes contact with the world of self-expression; through Adjaye, Ofili connects with that which is social and real. Where Ofili shies away from publicity, rarely giving interviews though generous with his interlocutors when he does, Adjaye is so completely at ease with the media that he has even become part of it, presenting both television and radio shows. He is assertive and charming, an ambassador for architecture as well as his own work. For both, being black has brought attention and, as they rise rapidly to the height of their professions, the mutual support they provide is hardly incidental.

If to look at their personalities is to see different characteristics, to look at their work is another matter. The unashamed excess of Ofili's work – he uses resin, oil, pencil, magazine cutouts and glitter and his work is layered both in construction and content – and the lush materiality of Adjaye's are not so far apart. Look at the outside of Tim Noble and Sue Webster's house, painted in a thick fudgy layer of bitumen paint – the same pointy-surfaced anti-flyposting paint you find on lampposts – it is tantalizing and repellent at the same time. In other projects, chipboard, honeycomb panelling and felt are used. But, as with Ofili's magnificent canvasses, the style only succeeds because the substance is there.

Ofili likes surfaces that are by turn shiny, mat, milky, opaque, sticky and clear. Adjaye does too. Consider the outside of the Idea Store in Chrisp Street, which is all brightly coloured glass on the outside and wholesomely woody within. Also, Lost House [pp 56–73], a sybaritic party apartment of black-painted timber, glass and mirror concealed behind an almost non-existent façade on a traffic-heavy street. Both play a highly selective game of sampling and reconfiguration, in which neither is afraid of luxe or beauty.

Ofili only worked in the studio at Fashion Street for two, maybe three, years. But, during that period and in that space, he produced a pivotal piece of work. He moved into the house after winning the Turner Prize in December 1998, the same year that he had an acclaimed show at the Serpentine Gallery. Tired of the pace and the pressure, and bored with the treadmill of 'making work one week and showing it the next', he hid in his studio producing a series of thirteen paintings of monkeys (*Mono 1 to 13*), derived from an Andy Warhol image of a monkey holding a cup. Each is a dramatic monochromatic statement, with monkey thirteen bigger and picked out in gold.

Most importantly, Ofili decided to turn his back on the tradition of the white-walled gallery to show this work. Together Adjaye and Ofili devised a context, a room, to be built in the Victoria Miro Gallery and any subsequent spaces where

CHRIS OFILI, UPPER ROOM, 2002

the paintings would be seen. The room's size and shape reflects those of the painting studio at Ofili's house. Located on the top floor of the gallery, they called it the Upper Room. There is, of course, a reference here to *The Last Supper*. Yet where *The Last Supper* is always viewed from the outside looking in, the Upper Room takes you to the heart of the action. First, you walk down a curving low-lit corridor lined in shimmering walnut veneer, and then into the space where the paintings, all identical but for their colour, glow like so many objets d'art around the walls. The sensation is one of being immersed in the work. It was an enormous critical success and Ofili had achieved his aim 'to enhance the experience of looking at art'. He had also made a significant shift from being a painter of 8-feet-high canvases to the creator (with Adjaye) of entire environments.

As a result of the critical acclaim, Ofili was invited to represent Britain at the Venice Biennale of 2003 and, with Adjaye, created a yet more elaborate context in which to show a luscious series of paintings about a pair of lovers in an earthly paradise on the island of Trinidad. The installation, a combination of thick carpets and deeply coloured walls, included a three-dimensional representation of the environment shown in the paintings: a kaleidoscopic explosion of red and green glass, reminiscent of church windows, nightclubs and Christmas decorations.

Painting the Upper Room series, Ofili realized that the restrictive width of the space made it difficult to work on bigger canvases and that he needed to move again to an outside studio. The disused studio in Fashion Street is in the process of being changed to a family room, its asceticism no longer relevant. Ofili's intimate relationship with the house has now had to dissolve to include other people; likewise Adjaye's relationship with Ofili.

As for that chance encounter in 1997, it ends with the Upper Room about to be installed permanently in London's Tate Modern. This is not a place that Ofili automatically assumed his work had a right to be, and much less Adjaye. Which architect would rightly see their work as destined for a fine art gallery?

The Upper Room is spectacular in its own right; that it is a product of two minds, of an ongoing debate between two men, adds to its sense of resolution. This substantial work is the eventual consequence of a dialogue that began between an architect and artist about the interior of a house.

Ofili House and Studio

project | 1998–99
total floor area | 247 SQ. M./2657 SQ. FT.
location | SPITALFIELDS, LONDON

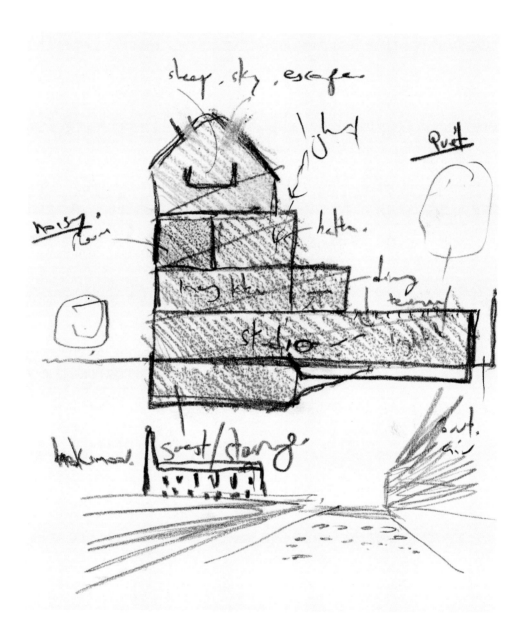

OCCUPYING THE SHELL of a Huguenot silk-weaver's house, which has considerable historic interest on its own account, the Ofili house and studio is situated in Spitalfields. The front façade is constructed from a close-jointed red brick, rather than London stock bricks, and terminates in a stepped gable, suggesting the Flemish origins of the first occupants. Apart from the staircase, which was carefully restored, the rest of the house was completely rebuilt.

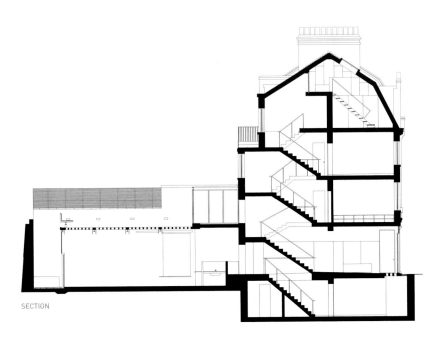

SECTION

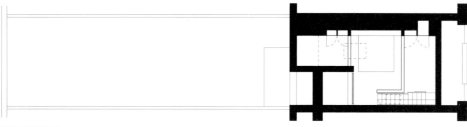

MEZZANINE PLAN

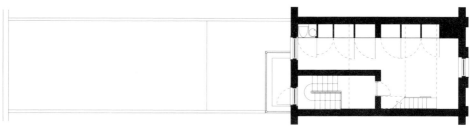

THIRD-FLOOR PLAN

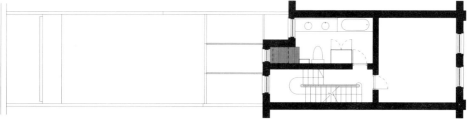

SECOND-FLOOR PLAN

Silk-weaving took place on the top floor where there was more natural light than at street level. At a later stage, the lower floors were used as a shop and a storage space was built in the garden. In the latest recycling, the storeroom has been rebuilt as a painting studio [pp 146–47] and the silk-weaving space has become the main bedroom with a sleeping gallery [p. 151]. On the street, the change of programme is signalled by a folding and sliding screen.

The studio receives natural light through the roof, constructed of glass blocks, and from a small court whose walls reflect sunlight through a glass screen. Artificial light is provided by fluorescent tubes and tungsten bulbs attached to the beams that support the roof.

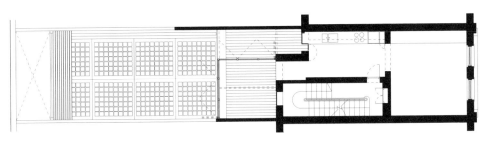

FIRST-FLOOR PLAN

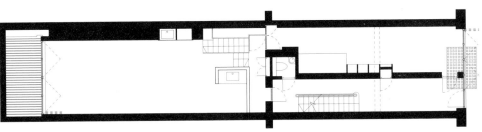

GROUND-FLOOR & STUDIO PLAN

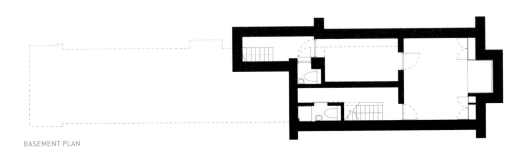

BASEMENT PLAN

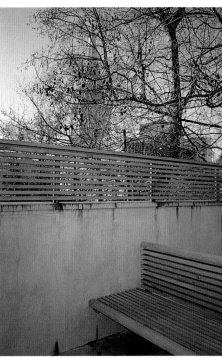

Compared with the verticality of the original house, the studio and living areas have been organized as horizontal sequences of carefully differentiated spaces. The kitchen occupies a gallery that connects a sitting area, looking over the street, with the dining area. A glass extension, the dining area opens directly onto the terrace formed by the roof of the studio and has a view of Christchurch Spitalfields, designed by Nicholas Hawksmoor, and the churchyard.

Inspired by the the materiality of the original staircase, the interior of the Ofili house is finished in natural (unpainted) plaster. It was necessary to continue the staircase into the basement and up to the mezzanine: the lower extension engages with the architecture of the studio space and has concrete treads between solid walls; the upper extension is constructed of steel and the handrail demonstrates a similar fluidity to its historic counterpart.

McGregor House

project   1998–2000
total floor area   453 SQ. M./4876 SQ. FT.
location   ST JOHN'S WOOD, LONDON

McGREGOR HOUSE OCCUPIES the shell of a semi-detached house in St John's Wood. The original house was constructed with shallow extensions to the side and back walls and Adjaye has linked these extensions at basement and ground-floor levels to form a new space that contains a staircase. Both the lower and upper sections of the rear extension have glazed roofs.

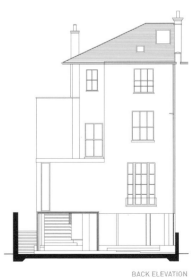

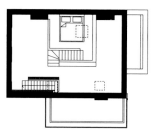

MEZZANINE PLAN

SECOND-FLOOR PLAN

FIRST-FLOOR PLAN

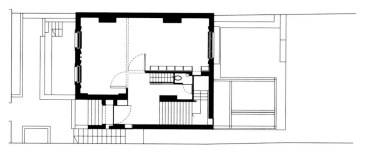

GROUND-FLOOR PLAN

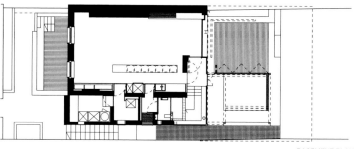

BASEMENT PLAN

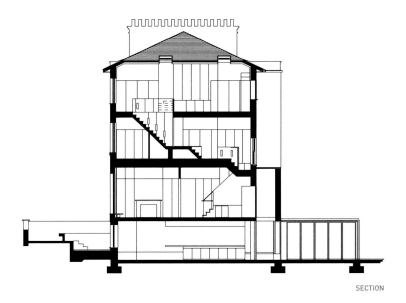

SECTION

There were several components to the conversion process. A new steel structure, working with the outer walls, made it possible to create larger, structure-free, spaces at all levels. Two entirely new volumes, a sleeping platform [p. 169] and a dining pavilion [p. 161], are located on the top floor and in the garden, respectively, and are connected with a running staircase. Finally, the space available within the outer shell has been reoccupied using a system based on fixed and moving panels.

The connection between the house and garden has been strengthened by cutting away the bottom section of the rear wall, supporting the wall above on two columns and glazing the remaining opening [opposite]. The dining pavilion was conceived as an over-scale porch, linking the foot of the staircase and the rest of the house with the garden. It also defines an open court, which takes its place within a spatial sequence starting at the front gate and ending at the rear wall of the site. Each stage of this route has been carefully delineated.

To improve the connection between the ground floor and the basement, two solid walls have been replaced with two glass panels to form one corner of the entrance hall. Apart from one vertical slot, the new rear wall is solid at this level, preventing a direct view into the garden. The main staircase descends into the basement between the glazed and solid walls and the roof of this space is constructed from a single double-glazed panel. In the kitchen, the stainless-steel detailing includes back-painted glass doors and back-lit panels, which figure in later projects.

With its self-consciously lined interiors and meandering staircase, McGregor House has more apparent parallels with the houses of Adolf Loos than other projects. Most spaces are lined with door-height vertical panels of MDF and are painted in a single colour. In positions where there may have been a structural corner in the original house, outward-opening doors dissolve the corner into thin air [opposite, bottom]. The vertical zoning of the house is reflected in changing floor finishes: terrazzo in the basement [p. 165], natural oak on the ground floor [opposite] and black oak on the floors above [above, p. 169].

The construction of the open space on the second floor involved placing a ring beam on top of the existing walls to prevent them from being pushed outwards when the roof was rebuilt without intermediate supports. The lower level of this space is extended upwards by the maple-clad volume of the dressing space and sleeping deck and horizontally by the top-lit bathing area containing two stone baths from Scotland. There is a roof terrace above the extension on the side of the house and the recessed slot above the bed exposes the brickwork of the original building.

Swarovski House

project | 2000–01
total floor area | 141 SQ.M./1517 SQ.FT.
location | ISLINGTON, LONDON

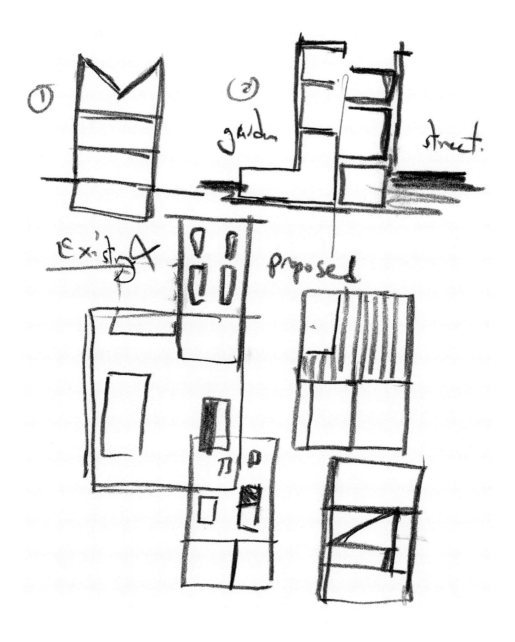

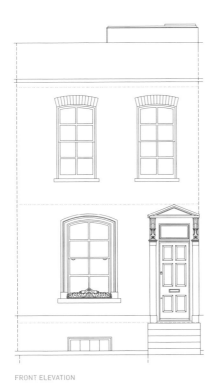

FRONT ELEVATION

THE WIDESPREAD CONSTRUCTION of basements in eighteenth- and nineteenth-century London was discussed by John Summerson in his book *Georgian London*. The earth from the basement was used to raise the level of the road, leaving a short flight of steps to the front door. The back garden, however, remained at its natural level but was not accessible from the reception rooms on the floor above. The reconfiguration of Swarovski House addresses this issue by placing a living space at basement level, which, due to its height, has a spatial connection with the front door.

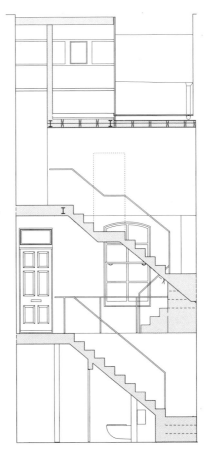

CROSS SECTION

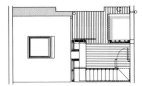

ROOF PLAN

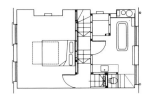

FIRST-FLOOR PLAN

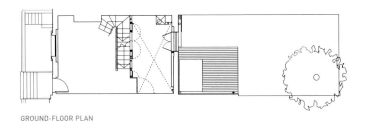

GROUND-FLOOR PLAN

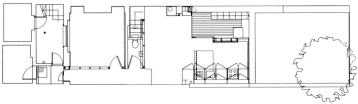

BASEMENT PLAN

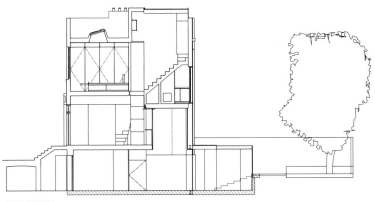

LONG SECTION

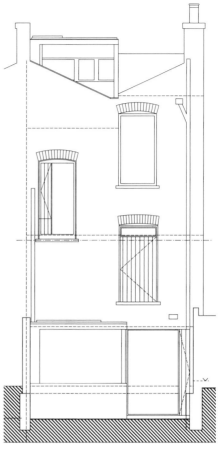

BACK ELEVATION

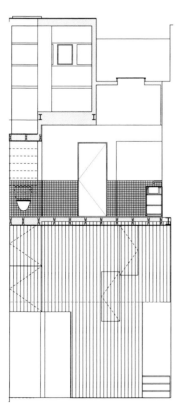

CROSS SECTION

In a London terrace house, the staircase forms a vertical element running through all floors and spatial interaction with the spaces it serves is limited, as in the case of the main staircase in the Ofili house. In Swarovski House, the staircase's containment, position and orientation is different at every level and its detailing is intimately linked with each of the spaces it serves. It forms a vertical *promenade architecturale*, connecting the basement to the roof.

Although the window openings of the original house have been retained, the rebuilding of the interior can be seen from the outside. From the street, the treads of a staircase are visible as they move in a transverse direction across the space that would previously have been the reception room [left], and, looking up, it is possible to see the sky through the new rooflight in the main bedroom. On the back façade, the floor of the new bathroom cuts across one window and lines up with the sill of another, so that a chair appears where convention suggests there should not be a floor for it to stand on. These interventions are more legible due to the replacement windows on the upper floors of the back wall.

Coming through the front door, a cranked staircase ascending into a top-lit space provides an immediate introduction to the themes of the house. The wall it stands against has three openings: the bathroom door on the landing, a window that slides past the the staircase itself, and a doorway onto a small internal balcony [above]. The window and the balcony introduce the internal architecture of the basement living space.

Unusually for a London terrace house, the two-storey basement space acknowledges each of the key levels resulting from the remodelling of the ground before the first construction began. With its exceptional height, boarded surfaces and the balcony and window on the inside wall, this could be an external space. It is unclear whether we should understand the house as an extension of the garden, or the garden as an extension of the house.

Above the living spaces, the bathroom and the main bedroom are positioned at intermediate levels on the way to the roof; both are integrated with the staircase as it winds its way upwards. The gain in height is marked by a change of material, birch plywood replacing oak boards. A small study at roof level [opposite] peeps over the butterfly-section parapet on the back façade, its exterior clad in Iroko timber.

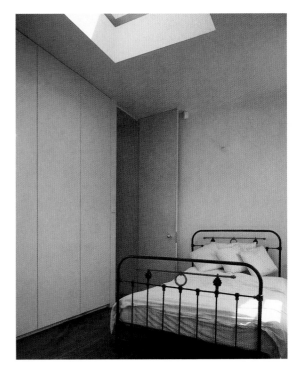

The use of rooflights to give levels of illumination comparable to an external space and the absence of visible window frames reinforce the sense of continuity between inside and outside. To this end, the significant roles played by other design elements have been suppressed. Without the new steel and timber structure that works with the original brick walls, the three-dimensional spiral of the house would not have been possible, but the existence of this structure has been masked by the continuous lining of the interior.

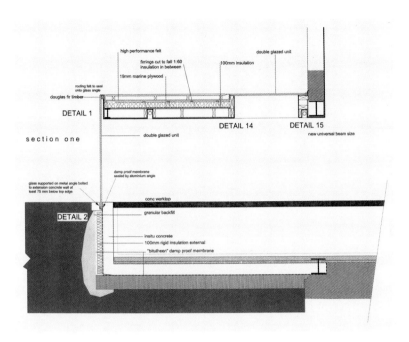

high performance felt

firrings cut to fall 1:60
insulation in between

19mm marine plywood

double glazed unit

100mm insulation

roofing felt to seal
onto glass angle

douglas fir timber

DETAIL 1

DETAIL 14

DETAIL 15

new universal beam size

section one

double glazed unit

glass supported on metal angle bolted
to extension concrete wall at
least 75 mm below top edge

damp proof membrane
sealed by aluminium angle

conc worktop

granular backfill

DETAIL 2

insitu concrete

100mm rigid insulation external

"bitutheen" damp proof membrane

CONSTRUCTION OF EXTENSION

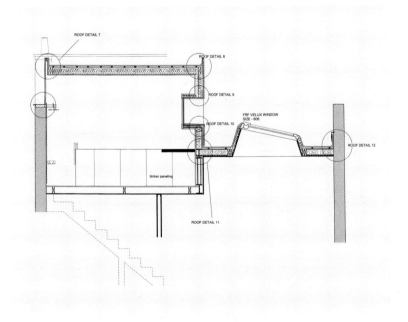

ROOF DETAIL 7

ROOF DETAIL 8

ROOF DETAIL 9

ROOF DETAIL 10

FRF VELUX WINDOW
SIZE - 606

ROOF DETAIL 12

timber paneling

ROOF DETAIL 11

CONSTRUCTION OF ROOF

BUILDING IN LONDON
Deyan Sudjic

There is a certain appealing worldliness about David Adjaye's architecture. It has an ambiguity to it that demonstrates his deft ability to have his cake and eat it. It is sparse but sensual, rooted in place but entirely cosmopolitan. It is serious in its intentions but easily accessible; you do not have to be an architect to get the point of his work. Indeed, there are times when he has been able, despite his affability, to succeed in getting up the noses of his primmer professional colleagues. When the Journal of the Royal Institute of British Architects put Adjaye's Elektra House on the cover, it provoked a flood of intemperately hostile correspondence that went on for months, with the institute's backwoodsmen wailing about what they saw as the hostility of its façade and the shortcomings they claimed to see in its construction.

Adjaye has been careful not to restrict himself to the conventional limits of architectural practice. He is not afraid to deal with the issue of fashion, without necessarily being seduced and entirely co-opted by it. And, he is as close to his contemporaries in the art world as any architect of his generation. He is driven by his interest in the material, physical qualities of architecture, rather than lapsing into virtuality or hermeneutics. Yet his work is informed by ideas as well as things. He is designing objects as well as environments.

Despite the fact that he was born to Ghanaian parents in Tanzania in the mid-1960s and moved around the world with his family before finally settling in Britain, he is an architect whose work could only be the product of the very particular circumstances of the London in which he was educated and began to practise in the 1990s. No European city has done more to reinvent itself in this period than London. It is a city going through a once-in-a-lifetime burst of growth and transformation on a scale of ambition not seen in Britain since the nineteenth century when London went through its last great period of metropolitan growth, with the huge expansion of the underground system, the completion of the mainline railway network and the cutting of such major new roads as Victoria Street and Shaftesbury Avenue through the existing urban fabric. Then, as now, a concentration of large-scale interventions transformed the geography of the city. It is in this context that the cumulative impact of individual projects needs to be understood.

In the 1980s, Canary Wharf, now a financial centre on a world scale, erupted from the site of a derelict banana warehouse in just five years, through a combination of the unforeseen use of tax subsidies, originally devised to encourage light industry within the city, and a relaxed planning regime. The glittering towers of Canary Wharf now loom over the brow-beaten East End streets in which Adjaye is building modestly scaled libraries and housing. A cross-channel rail link was dug in the 1990s, scores of new high-rises were planned. The transformation of a succession of run-down inner-city (as well as not so inner-city) slums from Clerkenwell to Hoxton saw the creation of a series of desirable new urban neighbourhoods that followed each other in quick succession. Business parks sprouted up around Heathrow. A new subway line was opened. Trams returned to the southern suburbs. Sites, left empty for decades, filled up, the derelict docks and railway marshalling yard made redundant by technological and economic change were taken in hand. The problem sites that seemed intractable and unfundable have been funded and built. The meanest buildings of the 1960s have been demolished and replaced on a scale that saw the streets of the Square Mile running and bubbling with mud churned up by construction, as sites from Paternoster to London Wall were comprehensively redeveloped for the second time in forty years. According to the mayor, Ken Livingstone, the city has even managed to reverse half a century of steady population decline to start growing in numbers again.

London has been reorganized and remodelled. It is a transformation that is having all kinds of unpredicted and unexpected effects, not least on the architects who work there. Adjaye belongs to a charmed generation that has not, so far, encountered the hard times that marked its predecessors. He has had the chance to build early and fairly extensively. Rather than retreat into the arcane confines of paper architecture that disdains building as a kind of defence mechanism, Adjaye has taken it for granted that he would be able to be more than a theoretical architect. That confidence has given him a kind of sunny optimism. His work has an innocent readiness to take risks and a relaxed reluctance to strike rhetorical attitudes. Disinclined to preach a manifesto, Adjaye has a painterly nonchalance about exploring themes in his work. Secure that there will be enough chances to test his ideas, he has experienced little temptation to try to do too much in just one project; rather, he has used his early schemes to investigate themes one at a time. Elektra House is about the creation of an interior world [pp 12–25]; the

Kensington penthouse apartment exploits the sensuousness of a rich material palette and flirts with Eileen Gray's refusal to fix spaces by treating them as mechanisms [pp 204–21].

The interior projects have lead directly to a series of commissions to design the artefacts needed to make them function: lamps, door handles, furniture. This work has reinforced Adjaye's easy way of dealing with the material qualities of his buildings and the way that they are put together. Detail for Adjaye is not a fetishistic attempt to create the precision of jewelry. However, he does have a flair for dealing with these issues.

A decade ago, London would not have made a very likely candidate as Europe's leading centre for art. Tate Modern, the Turner Prize and the city's constellation of prospering artists have decisively changed that perception. There is now not only a thriving community of well-regarded artists, but also a market for their work and a network of galleries to show and sell it. A decade ago, despite the legacy of the 1960s, London would not have been regarded as a city with a larger contribution to make to contemporary fashion than Milan; Alexander McQueen, Stella McCartney and others suggest that this perception is also changing. Adjaye is part of those worlds and has helped to make architecture part of a wider conversation. He has designed studios, fashion shops, bars and exhibition spaces, the infrastructure that forms the backdrop to a very particular strand of London life, a life he shapes as well as reflects. In that sense, Adjaye is responsible for the architectural soundtrack to Hoxton. That is not to suggest that Adjaye is only interested in the surfaces of things; his work has substance as well as stylistic self-confidence. In many ways, Adjaye's approach has been shaped by the cultural flowering that London has gone through.

Perhaps London does not let its architects do their best work at home, but it is proving more than usually open to new definitions of urbanism and architecture. After years of stagnation, contemporary architecture, which, for a variety of reasons, was at the very outermost edge of Britain's cultural preoccupations, has started to take on a much less marginal position. As the work has grown more sophisticated, so has its audience – it is no longer entirely unheard of for City bonuses to be spent on hard-core architecture. The IKEA television advertising campaign urging us to chuck out the chintz actually seems to have worked.

London has prospered, and turned into an ever more cosmopolitan city, which has begun to invest heavily in public transport and its primary and secondary schools. But, there are costs, its hospitals are only kept functioning by poaching qualified doctors and nurses from African and Asian nations that can ill afford to loose them. And, while London is a more tolerant society than it has ever been, it is still a city in which the old panic at the presence of outsiders surfaces from time to time in the shrill hysteria about asylum seekers. Also, the obverse side of rampant property inflation is the inability of the vast majority of its population to find a place to live within its central zones.

Adjaye operates at both ends of that spectrum without skipping a beat, working for wealthy bankers and designing libraries for the children of the very poor. He is in the provocative position of operating on the edge of the world of celebrity and addressing the concerns of an East End local authority looking for fresh ways of embracing the needs of disadvantaged communities. Adjaye's libraries for Tower Hamlets – known as Idea Stores – are able to bring a gloss of sophistication to the normally defiantly plain world of local government services, certainly no handicap for an organization that is attempting to bring back young people to the world of learning. The Idea Stores are injections of a renewed energy into the worn-down East End, a promise that the transformations of the market economy have not entirely passed by the people of the area.

The particular circumstances of London in the late 1990s and the early years of the twenty-first century – the unprecedented building boom and the burst of creative energy in art, music and fashion – served to shape Adjaye's career. He began by designing a series of predominantly low-budget studios for a succession of young artists, including Chris Ofili and Jake Chapman. He went on to work on a joint project for an arts centre with Ofili, who is best known for his preoccupation with the unorthodox use of materials, and then collaborated on the artist's installation for the British pavilion at the Venice Biennale in 2003. It is a relationship that has clearly marked Adjaye's work and has given it a distinctive flavour. Adjaye makes the most of the materials he can afford and has reintroduced some sense of the physical qualities that have been lost from much contemporary architecture. He makes buildings that invite you to touch and feel them and in which you are made aware of the thickness of a wall, or the tightness of the space confined by a light shaft or a staircase.

Interested in the sense of oscillation that is set up by the tension between rough and smooth, hot and cold, Adjaye's early projects were the product of London's battered and grimy streets. He manages to bring together sheen and grit

ROOF VIEW FROM THE IDEA STORE ON CHRISP STREET TO CANARY WHARF

to create a surreal dislocation that is rooted in the familiar but also capable of jolting us out of the ordinary. Elektra House, for example, is sited on a pinched East End terraced street, replete with weathered late-Georgian brickwork, sash windows and panelled doors. The regular pattern of glass and brick set up by the rest of the street is abruptly halted by a mysterious brooding black obelisk. The smooth, shiny skin is actually specially treated plywood, although it could equally well be steel or lead, an ambiguity that increases its exotic quality. Inside the house, the cramped realities of Whitechapel street life slip away as the interior is configured to present carefully framed views of the world. However, Adjaye did not create the blank street front in a perverse attempt at contextualism or even for security reasons. His clients wanted to be able to use the ground floor as a gallery-like space in which to make and show large-scale artworks, but also wanted to be able to live above them.

The last time that London was home to a whole generation of artists affluent enough to commission architects to design studios for them, Queen Victoria was still young and the Pre-Raphaelites were a huge popular success. In 1865, for example, Lord Leighton asked George Aitchison to build an Italianate villa for him in Kensington, then something of an artist's colony. There were several clusters of studio houses within walking distance, distinguished by their north-facing studio windows and the specially designed slot-like wall openings intended to facilitate the removal of extra-large canvasses. Aitchison designed the house to reflect the style of Leighton's paintings. The plan unconsciously reflected the social place of the artist in the Victorian hierarchy, with a back door for models so that they could come and go without disturbing Leighton's clients, who were greeted at the front door.

Money made during the current London art boom has re-created a similar situation. This time however, it is in the east of the city, in Hoxton and Stepney that London's new artists' quarter is taking shape. Jay Jopling's White Cube Gallery in Hoxton Square, with a glass roof that makes it look like a colonial outpost of Tate Modern, is in walking distance of a series of newly built artists' studios. David Adjaye's Dirty House for the artists Sue Webster and Tim Noble may speak a very different architectural language from Aitchison's but it too reflects the artistic preoccupations of his clients.

Having proven himself an adept designer of small spaces that have distinctive qualities, Adjaye is now working on larger-scale and more far-flung projects, as in his series of libraries in London and the art gallery in Denver. Jumping to this scale is a risk of course. Adjaye has covered a lot of ground very quickly. He is in the midst of demonstrating that he is capable of moving on from his roots in London, which have had such an impact on his work. But then architecture always needs to take risks.

project | 1998
total floor area | 206 SQ. M./2217 SQ. FT.
location | ST JOHN'S WOOD, LONDON

THE RELATIONSHIP BETWEEN a semi-detached house (listed Grade II for its historic interest) and garden in an inner London suburb is reconfigured in this project. The back wall of the main house has been cut away at basement level, leaving the wall above supported on a concrete beam. This is the most far-reaching element of the design. In anticipation of a strategy developed in later projects, the floor above was substantially rebuilt.

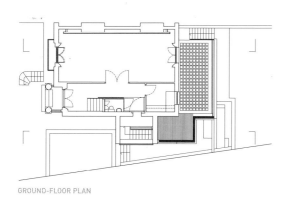

GROUND-FLOOR PLAN

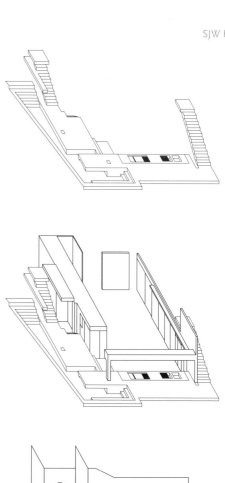

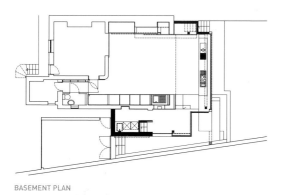

BASEMENT PLAN

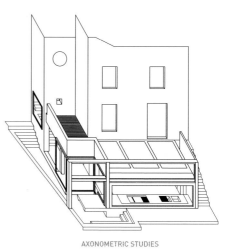

AXONOMETRIC STUDIES

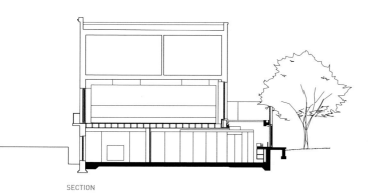

SECTION

The new basement houses a kitchen and day room. The extension increases the ceiling height and, with the use of glass blocks to admit light from above, improves the spatial qualities of the basement as a whole. The kitchen worktop continues the plane of the ground into the new space.

On the floor above basement level, the extension forms a terrace that is accessible from the reception room. The height of the glass balustrade is identical to that of the kitchen window, which can be raised and lowered by hydraulic jacks. When it is open [p. 200], it lines up with the balustrade and the basement and garden become a single space that, in terms of form, can be equally appreciated from inside or outside. Adjaye observed this type of equivalence in the relationship between certain temples and their garden spaces in Kyoto.

A significant aspect of the new work is the degree to which it enhances the visual characteristics of the original house. In terms of structure, the project includes substantial concrete columns and beams to deal with the increased loads. The physical weight of these components is dissipated by a screen of galvanized steel columns that supports the motorized window and frames the main route into the garden. The spatial definition of the basement is supported by two storage walls, and the connection with the garden is articulated by using concrete to form an architectural landscape on both sides of the external wall.

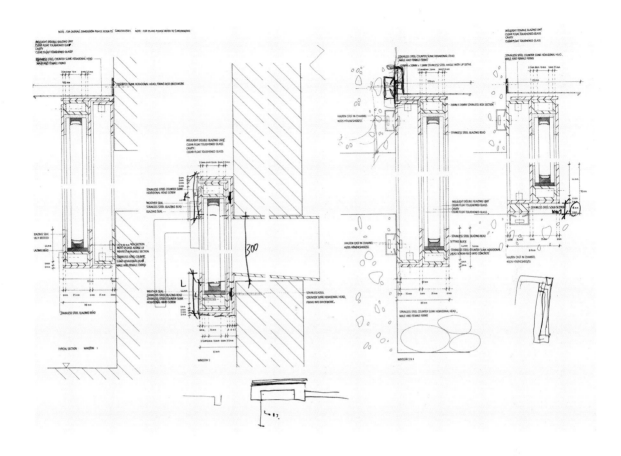

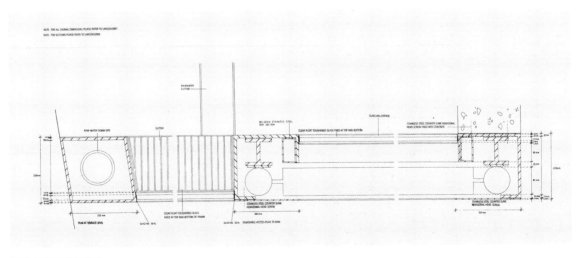

DETAILS OF CONSTRUCTION

KPG House

project	1998 – 2001
total floor area	439 SQ. M./4728 SQ. FT.
location	KENSINGTON, LONDON

IN EFFECT, KPG HOUSE is a new single-storey building standing on the roof of a stone-clad apartment block overlooking Kensington Palace Gardens. Situated in a conservation area, the house's exterior had to be designed as a sympathetic extension to the earlier structure, and it is for this reason that the steel frame of the new house is contained within the depth of the new construction. The main elevations are fully glazed, but nonetheless the construction of the roof includes a series of rooflights whose scale and cross section are closely related to the spaces they serve.

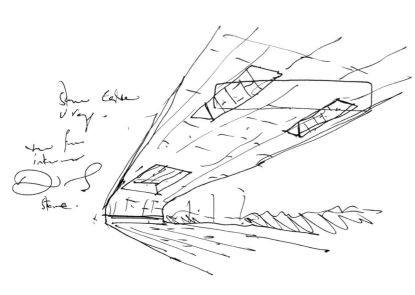

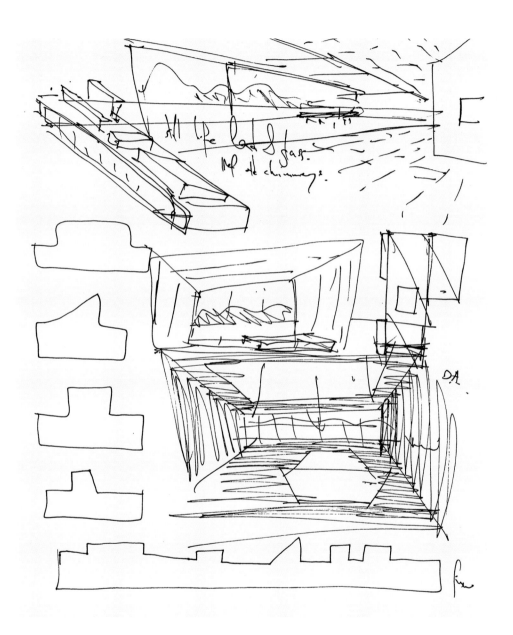

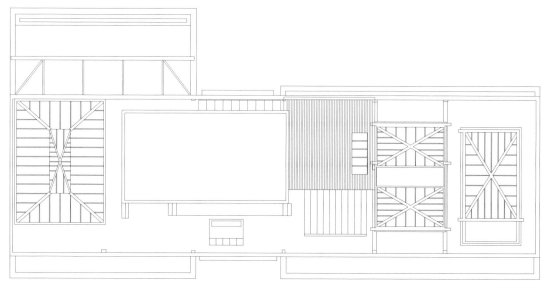

ROOF PLAN

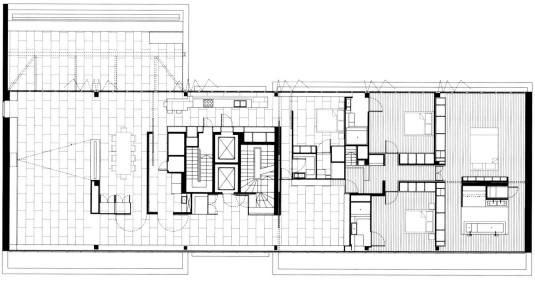

FLOOR PLAN

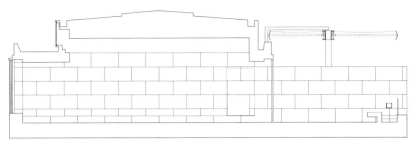

SECTION THROUGH LIVING ROOM AND TERRACE

In his book *The Poetics of Space*, Gaston Bachelard suggests that houses should be at least three or four stories high so that there is a clear difference between the bottom and top floors, the cellar and the garret. In this house, Adjaye has made a similar distinction on a horizontal basis by separating the more public spaces, which are lined with limestone [pp 212–13], from the more private areas, which are lined with various kinds of timber [pp 217–20]. In the middle, there is a transitional zone occupied by the butler's bedroom and the library: these spaces have stone floors and timber-lined walls [p. 216].

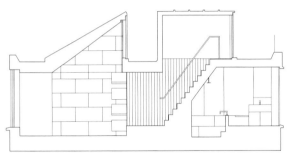

SECTION THROUGH LIBRARY

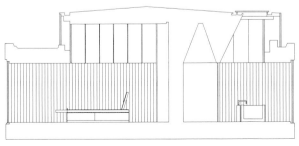

SECTION THROUGH MASTER BEDROOM

The passenger lift opens onto a long west-facing gallery, connecting the main reception space to the library, and the point of entry is marked by a dramatic rooflight [opposite]. The public areas are lined with thin sheets of limestone mounted on an aluminium honeycomb backing to save stone and reduce weight. The horizontal recessed slots on some walls suggest that the stone does not have a structural function.

The west elevation forms a continuous glazed wall of Priva-lite that can be changed from translucent to transparent by the throw of a switch, which triggers an electrical current to pass through the gas contained in the void between the inner and outer faces of each panel. In contrast, the east elevation employs a system of folding and sliding glazed panels. Opposite the reception and dining spaces, the panels open onto a roof terrace where a steel arch supports a retractable canopy. When the canopy is not in use, the arch frames the view in this direction.

To accommodate drainage from the bathrooms, the floor of the private areas is slightly higher than in the public spaces. The change in ceiling height between the public and private areas is a further difference, as is the more frequent use of rooflights in the private space to compensate for the lower ceiling. The library walls and shelves are constructed from smoked oak and the front edges of the shelves incorporate fibre-optic lighting [above and right].

Due to the service void below, the floor of the bedrooms is at the same level as the top of the parapet of the older building. On the west side, the glazed panels slide to one side leaving a clear view of the park. The walls and furniture in the guest bedrooms are finished in sycamore, and the bathrooms, including the tubs and basins, are lined in a water-resistant bituminous limestone.

The master suite, with bedroom and bathroom on opposite sides of the building, is finished in ebony. The rooflights fulfil a double function: during the day, they admit indirect light that balances the light from the glazed walls; at night, their translucent surfaces are illuminated by artificial light, creating a dramatic vertical extension to the space below.

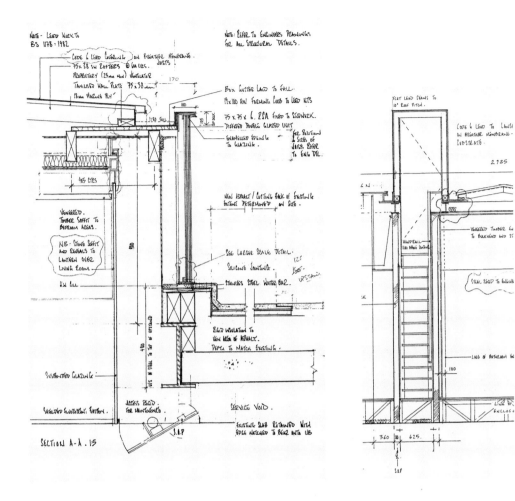

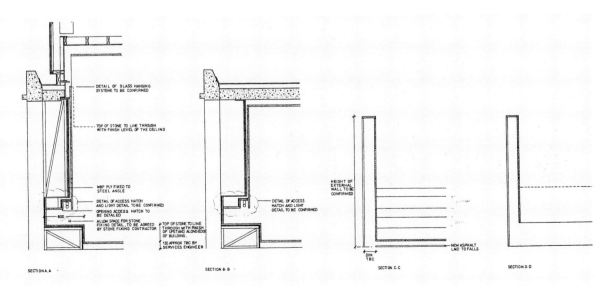

SECTION A.A. SECTION B-B SECTION C-C SECTION D-D

BAR House

project | 2000–03
total floor area | 269 SQ. M./2894 SQ. FT.
location | ISLINGTON, LONDON

THIRD-FLOOR PLAN

SECOND-FLOOR PLAN

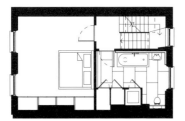

FIRST-FLOOR PLAN

WHEN THIS FOUR-STOREY TERRACE house, plus basement, was first constructed, the ground levels were adjusted (as in Swarovski House). The floor levels in BAR House have not been changed, but the relationship with the ground has been transformed by excavating the garden to the same level as the basement. A dining area extends the basement into the garden, and, when the glazed wall is pivoted upwards, the basement and garden become a single space [p. 230, left].

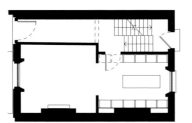

GROUND-FLOOR PLAN

BASEMENT PLAN

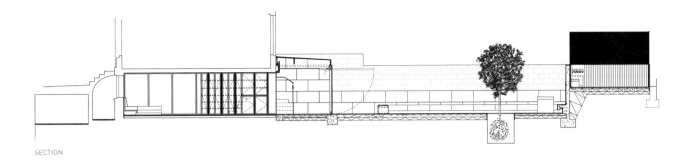

SECTION

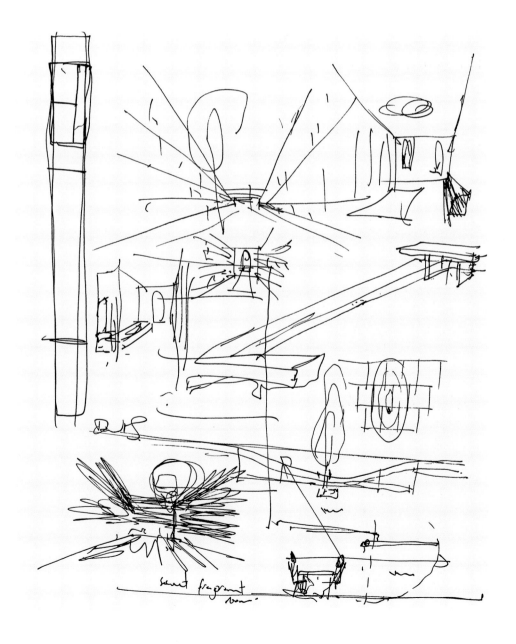

The kitchen worktop connects the sitting area at the front of the house with the dining space and garden; for continuity, the floors and walls of each of these spaces are lined with black basalt [pp 228–29]. The existing staircase has been retained, although one section was in such poor condition it had to be rebuilt. An additional flight of steps links the main staircase to the dining area and gives an elevated view of the garden [above].

The garden has some similarities with Concrete Garden [pp 100–07]: they are both spaces that have been deliberately vacated, and, by contrasting with their surroundings, they take on a greater clarity. In this case, however, nature has begun to make a comeback – a small fountain and a birch tree break through the pavement, and a bent rectangular tube, of a kind that figures in other projects, forms the seating for a stone table and the long trough for further planting. A boarded area at the end of the garden is at natural ground level.

Compared with the transformation of the basement and garden, the strategy on the other floors is one of restoration and sensitive upgrading. All floor finishes have been renewed, and in the library and bathrooms there is a careful balance between the architecture of the original house and the new work. In the bedrooms, the design of the storage walls takes into account the proportions of each space.

Works

3

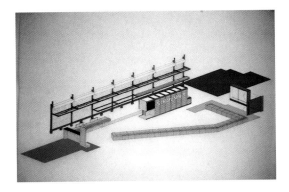

1995	Set Design for *The Pretenders* London, UK	
1995	Schlotsky's London, UK	1
1995	Wilson Apartment London, UK	2
1996	Soba Noodle Bar London, UK	3
1997	Lunch @ Exmouth Market London, UK	4
1998	Newton House London, UK	

5

6

7

8

| 1998– | Whitehall Apartment   8 |
| 1999 | London, UK |

| 1998– | Ofili House and Studio |
| 1999 | London, UK |

| 1999 | Social Bar and Club   9 |
| | London, UK |

1999	Crafts Council
	London, UK
	'(Un)Limited'
	Exhibition Design

1999	The London Institute
	London, UK
	'Future Map'
	Exhibition Design

| 1999 | Bazaar Boutique |
| | London, UK |

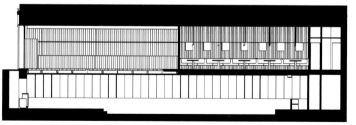

9

10

<table>
</table>

1999   Shada Pavilion   10
        London, UK
        Collaboration with
        Henna Nadeem

1999   Jake Chapman
        House and Gallery   11
        London, UK

2000   Crafts Council
        London, UK
        'RIPE'
        Exhibition Design

2000   Boardroom for
        The Guardian
        Newspaper HQ   12
        London, UK

1998–   Elektra House
2000   London, UK

11

12

13

14

16

2001　Ellen Gallagher
Jungle Gym　15
New York, USA
Design of art installation
pictured here at the
Drawing Center

2001　Crafts Council
London, UK
Jerwood Prize, Applied Arts
Exhibition Design

2001　Sainsbury House
London, UK

2001–　Dirty House
2002　London, UK

1999–　Folkestone Library　16
2002　Folkestone, Kent, UK
Collaboration with
Chris Ofili and Shin
and Tomoko Azumi

2001–　Glass House
2002　London, UK

15

17

18

19

20

2002   Selfridges Manchester 20
        Manchester, UK
        Beauty and Accessories Hall

2002–   11–29 Fashion Street 21
2003   London, UK
        Office and Retail Development

21

2003   Barbican Curve Gallery
        London, UK
        'Witness'
        Exhibition Design

2003   Selfridges: Women's
        Superbrand Zone 22
        London, UK

2000–   BAR House
2003   London, UK

22

24

25

26

23

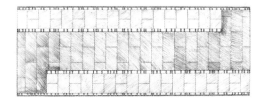

27

28

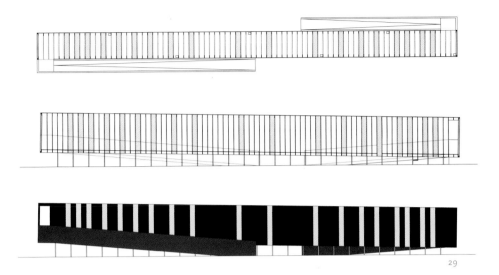

29

2004	L x W x H 29	
	London, UK	
	Architectural Installation Commissioned by the Institute of International Visual Arts (inIVA)	
2004	Victoria & Albert Museum	
	London, UK	
	'Black British Style' Exhibition Design	
2004	Frieze Art Fair	
	London, UK	
2003– 2004	Angelika Apartment	
	Berlin, Germany	
2002– 2004	Lost House	
	London, UK	
2003– 2004	Abbey 30	
	UK	
	Architectural Rebranding of Retail Network	

30

31

32

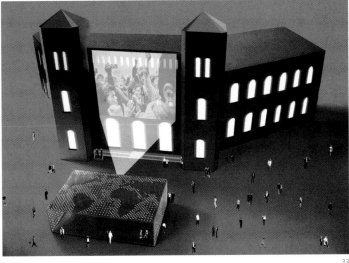
33

34

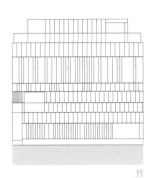

35

36

37

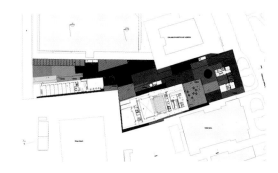

38

39

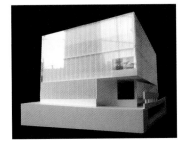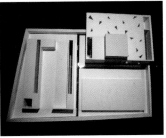

40

BIOGRAPHICAL NOTES

Born in Dar–Es–Salaam, Tanzania to Ghanaian parents on 22 September, 1966.

Lives in Middle East and Africa, 1966–78.

Moves to London, UK, 1979.

Attends Middlesex University and receives a Diploma in Art and Design, 1985–86.

Works in the offices of Chassay Architects, London, 1988–90.

Attends Southbank University and receives BA Hons Architecture RIBA Part I. Writes dissertation, 'Shibam, City in the Desert, Yemen', 1989–90.

Wins First Prize Bronze Medal from Royal Institute of British Architects, 1990.

Works in the offices of David Chipperfield Architects, London, 1991.

Works in the offices of Eduardo Souto de Moura Architects, Portugal, 1991.

Attends Royal College of Art and receives MA Architecture RIBA Part II. Writes dissertation, 'Sacred Place and Tea Ceremony in Japan', 1991–93.

Teaches at South Bank University, 1993–2002.

Starts architectural practice with William Russell, 1994.

Receives his RIBA Part III, and becomes ARB registered, 1997.

Teaches at Royal College of Art, 1998–2002.

Reforms his practice as Adjaye/Associates, 2000.

Presents *Dreamspaces* series on modern architecture for BBC: Series I, 2002; Series II, 2003.

Interviews Oscar Niemeyer in Brazil for BBC Radio 4, 2004.

Teaches at Architectural Association, 2003–05.

Selected Lectures

Harvard's Graduate School of Design, Cambridge, MA, 2001.

University of Hanover, Germany, 2001.

Dulwich Picture Gallery, London, UK, 2001.

Universidad de Luisdad in Lisbon, Portugal, 2001.

Cornell University, Ithaca, NY, 2002.

Cambridge University, UK, 2002.

Yale University, New Haven, CT, 2003.

Art Center College of Design, Los Angeles, CA, 2003.

The Tate, Liverpool, UK, 2003.

Royal College of Art, London, UK, 2004.

Norsk Forum, Oslo, Norway, 2004.

Architecture Congress, Monterrey, Mexico, 2004.

CCAC, San Francisco, CA, 2004.

Univeristy of California-Berkeley, CA, 2004.

Royal Academy, London, UK, 2004.

Selected Exhibitions/Recognition

'Outside/In: London Architecture', Architeckturforum, Innsbruck, Austria, 2000.

'Space Invaders', British Council, 2001.

'Next', Venice Biennale of Architecture, 2002.

World Architecture Awards, Best European House, Elektra House, 2002.

São Paulo Bienal, Brazil, 2003.

Advisor to the London Development Agency, Thames Gateway Design Panel, 2003–05.

'Metamorph', Venice Biennale of Architecture, 2004.

'Recent Work of Emerging Architects', GA Gallery, Tokyo, Japan, 2004.

CREDITS

Contributors

Peter Allison, Editor
The curator of recent exhibitions on Austrian architecture and new architecture from London, Peter Allison also contributes to a number of international publications on architecture. He teaches in London.

Stuart Hall
A writer and cultural theorist, Stuart Hall is an Associate Fellow on the Cross Cultural Contemporary Arts Project at Goldsmiths College, University of London, and a board member of inIVA and Autograph.

Caroline Roux
Specializing in design, Caroline Roux is a writer and columnist at *The Guardian* newspaper. She met David Adjaye when he completed his first sandwich bar in 1995 and has written about his work regularly ever since.

Deyan Sudjic
A former editor of *Domus* and *Blueprint*, Deyan Sudjic is the architecture critic for *The Observer* newspaper in London. He was director of the Venice Architecture Biennale in 2002 and also of 'Glasgow 1999, UK City of Architecture and Design'.

Image Credits

Unless otherwise indicated, all sketches, models, computer-generated images and photographs created by Adjaye/Associates.

All photographs of house projects by Lyndon Douglas

With the exception of:
Glass House [pp 108–17]: Nikolai Delvendahl
Ofili House and Studio [pp 138–53] and
SJW House [pp 192–203]: Ed Reeve

Additional Credits

A–Models: model p. 250 [36]
Cameraphoto, Venezia: p. 245
Kei–Lu Choang: illustration p. 249 [34]
Lyndon Douglas: pp 80–81, 119, 122, 124 [bottom], 125 [top], 126–27, 130–31, 238, 239 [12], 240, 241 [16], 242, 243 [21 + 22], 244 [25 + 26], 246 [27]
Miller Hare: illustration p. 249 [33]
Sal Idriss: p. 79
Richard Learoyd: p. 236 [5]
J. Littkeman: p. 244 [24]
Magali Moreau: pp 76–77, 84, 234, 235 [4]
Ed Reeve: pp 78, 120–21, 123, 124 [top], 125 [bottom], 128–29, 236 [6 + 7], 237 [8 + 9]
Toni Yli–Suvanto Studio: illustration p. 249 [33]
Digital video images captured from the video installation, *31*, by Lorna Simpson, p. 241 [15]

Projects listed on pp 234–37: Adjaye & Russell

Copyright

Unless otherwise indicated, all sketches, models, computer-generated images and photographs by Adjaye/Associates are ©Adjaye/Associates, London, 2004.

Individual copyrights retained by the photographers: ©Cameraphoto, Venezia, ©Lyndon Douglas, ©Sal Idriss, ©Richard Learoyd, ©Magali Moreau, ©Ed Reeve.

Aerial views of London, courtesy of Getmapping, www.getmapping.com.

Page 86 © Tate, London 2005

Publication

Concept and design: Adjaye/Associates
Art direction: Karen Wong
Design: Avni Patel
Pre-press: Hannah Booth

First published in the United Kingdom in 2005 by
Thames & Hudson Ltd,
181A High Holborn,
London WC1V 7QX

www.thamesandhudson.com

British Library Cataloguing-in-Publication Data
A catalogue record for this book is available from the
British Library

ISBN-13: 978-0-500-34205-3
ISBN-10: 0-500-34205-9

Printed and bound in China by Toppan Printing Co. Ltd.